500 RECIPES
FOR MEAT DISHES

by Marguerite Patten

HAMLYN

Contents

Introduction

In this book you will find the basic methods of cooking meat to obtain the very best result. Undoubtedly meat is one of the most expensive items on the family budget, and it is therefore a food that should be bought with thought, with a certain amount of knowledge and with an idea of the week's menus ahead.

Families tend to be a little conservative about their methods of cooking meat. They choose roast joints and grills, often forgetting that casserole dishes are delicious, that a very little wine is not particularly extravagant, and it does help to tenderize the meat, that fruit is not only good as a sauce to accompany meat but excellent put into the dish itself.

You will find there are a number of new treatments of meat, as well as the basic techniques of choosing, keeping and cooking meat. The recipes serve four people unless otherwise stated.

I hope you will find this book of value in your catering, both for your family and when you entertain.

Cover photograph by Paul Williams

Published by Hamlyn Publishing,
a division of The Hamlyn Publishing Group Limited,
Bridge House, London Road, Twickenham,
Middlesex, England

Revised edition 1971
Thirteenth impression 1985

ISBN 0 600 36020 2

Printed and bound in Great Britain by
R. J. Acford

Useful Facts and Figures

Notes on metrication

In case you wish to convert quantities into metric measures, the following tables give a comparison.

Solid measures

Ounces	Approx. grams to nearest whole figure	Recommended conversion to nearest unit of 25
1	28	25
2	57	50
3	85	75
4	113	100
5	142	150
6	170	175
7	198	200
8	227	225
9	255	250
10	283	275
11	312	300
12	340	350
13	368	375
14	396	400
15	425	425
16 (1 lb)	454	450
17	482	475
18	510	500
19	539	550
20 (1¼ lb)	567	575

Note: When converting quantities over 20 oz first add the appropriate figures in the centre column, then adjust to the nearest unit of 25. As a general guide, 1 kg (1000 g) equals 2·2 lb or about 2 lb 3 oz. This method of conversion gives good results in nearly all cases, although in certain pastry and cake recipes a more accurate conversion is necessary to produce a balanced recipe.

Liquid measures

Imperial	Approx. millilitres to nearest whole figure	Recommended millilitres
¼ pint	142	150
½ pint	283	300
¾ pint	425	450
1 pint	567	600
1½ pints	851	900
1¾ pints	992	1000 (1 litre)

Oven temperatures

The table below gives recommended equivalents.

	°C	°F	Gas Mark
Very cool	110	225	¼
	120	250	½
Cool	140	275	1
	150	300	2
Moderate	160	325	3
	180	350	4
Moderately hot	190	375	5
	200	400	6
Hot	220	425	7
	230	450	8
Very hot	240	475	9

Notes for American and Australian users

In America the 8-oz measuring cup is used. In Australia metric measures are now used in conjunction with the standard 250-ml measuring cup. The Imperial pint, used in Britain and Australia, is 20 fl oz, while the American pint is 16 fl oz. It is important to remember that the Australian tablespoon differs from both the British and American tablespoons; the table below gives a comparison. The British standard tablespoon, which has been used throughout this book, holds 17·7 ml, the American 14·2 ml, and the Australian 20 ml. A teaspoon holds approximately 5 ml in all three countries.

To Buy Meat

Meat is undoubtedly at its best when freshly cooked. Re-heating meat takes away some of the flavour, and in some cases can make the meat a little dry, unless great care is taken. It is therefore unwise to buy very large joints of meat, thinking they can be used up afterwards, unless you are fond of cold meat, or enjoy dishes such as rissoles and shepherd's pie.

On the other hand, if you are a small family, a tiny joint of meat can often contain a bone which is out of proportion to the amount of the edible meat, and in this way it does become extravagant. The wise shopper finds the happy medium, a joint that is big enough to cook without having too much left over.

Obviously, you will not always be buying joints, and this is where money can be saved by adding to your knowledge of how to use cheaper pieces of meat for casseroling, grilling or even for slow roasting.

The following points give an idea of the quantities of meat you should allow. The amount of meat people consume varies a great deal. In some countries, Australia in particular, a tradition of meat-eating has been established and the quantities given here would be considered a minimum; the following will be a good guide:

Stewing Allow 4–6 oz. meat per person, weight without bone. Vegetables added to a stew help it to be filling.

Grilling Allow one good-sized chop or two small chops or cutlets per person, 4–8 oz. steak per person.

Roasting For a small joint with a large bone allow approximately 10–12 oz. per person. For a larger joint, where the bone is proportionately smaller, allow 8oz. meat per person, or less if stuffing the joint.

Salted meats These tend to shrink more when cooked than fresh meats, so be a little more generous with quantities allowed.

Cooked meats Allow 3–4 oz. per person.

In some recipes the quantities allowed per person may seem unusually large or small compared with the average helping. This is because the meat is either one that is easily digested and more can be eaten, or, as in some of the pork recipes, is rich and fatty and rather less than normal can be eaten.

How to tell if meat is fresh

First and foremost be selective about your butcher. If you are moving to a new town and choosing a butcher look carefully to see how the meat is displayed, how the shop is kept, whether the assistants look clean and immaculate. All this is a guide to whether or not the butcher takes a pride in selling really first-class meat.

The following points will give you an idea how meat should be judged for freshness.

Beef

1 The lean should be a clear bright red and the fat firm and pale cream.
2 The very best joints MUST have a certain amount of fat on them.

Mutton or lamb

1 The lean should be a dull red, but very firm, and the fat should be white.
2 Lamb is paler in colour than mutton. In many recipes either can be used. When stewing, mutton takes longer to cook.

Veal

1 The lean should be pale pink and look dry. There is little fat to see, but what there is should be firm and white.
2 Be very critical, particularly in hot weather, as veal does not keep well.

Pork

1 The lean should be pale pink and the fat white and dry.
2 Pork must never be served underdone.
3 Avoid serving it in very hot weather.

Bacon and ham

1 See that bacon looks moist and not too dry.
2 Bacon may be blanched or soaked to remove excess salt before adding to other dishes, so do not refuse slightly salted bacons.
3 Do not confuse ham and bacon—they have been cured in entirely different ways.

Offal

1 Liver, heart and kidneys should smell fresh and be firm in texture.
2 Sweetbreads and tripe should be white and not dull in appearance.

Cooked meats

1 These should look bright, not dull in colour.
2 They should not be hard in texture, this shows staleness.
3 They should smell fresh and pleasant.

To Keep Meat

If you have a refrigerator that is the correct place to keep meat.

1 Unwrap the meat and put it in the chiller tray under the freezing compartment if the piece is not too large.

2 If the meat is too big to go into this tray keep the meat on a plate towards the top of the cabinet, which is the coolest place.

3 Raw meat is on the whole best left uncovered, although with very lean meat, such as veal or fillet steak, there is a tendency for the outside to harden if kept for any length of time. A piece of foil, polythene or greaseproof paper can be put lightly over it.

4 Once meat has been cooked, it should always be covered before storing in the refrigerator.

5 If you are keeping a lot of meat in a refrigerator make certain that there is adequate air circulation round it; otherwise if the air does not circulate properly the meat will spoil in time.

To keep meat without a refrigerator

1 Make certain that you are putting the meat somewhere where flies cannot get to it. The old-fashioned meat-safe is quite a good idea, except that it is better to stand meat on a trivet over a plate rather than on a plate. In this way the air can circulate round, and the perforated meat-safe allows free entry of air.

2 If you do not have a meat-safe stand the meat on a plate in cold water, cover with paper or muslin.

3 In hot weather the best way to keep meat is to tie it in a piece of strong muslin and hang it from a shelf. In this way the air circulation is good and the meat is protected from flies, etc.

4 Choose the coldest place for meat at all times, for even in winter quite a lot of heat penetrates into a pantry from the cooker.

5 In hot weather, particularly, it is a good idea to wipe the meat with a little cold water and vinegar before storing.

6 Before cooking meat do wash or wipe it well, for it will have received considerable handling before it comes to your kitchen.

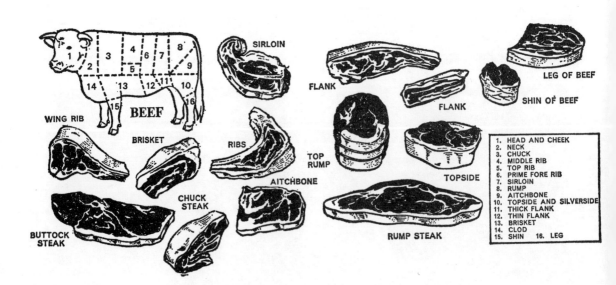

SIRLOIN

FLANK

FLANK

LEG OF BEEF

SHIN OF BEEF

WING RIB

BEEF

BRISKET

RIBS

TOP RUMP

AITCHBONE

TOPSIDE

CHUCK STEAK

BUTTOCK STEAK

RUMP STEAK

1. HEAD AND CHEEK
2. NECK
3. CHUCK
4. MIDDLE RIB
5. TOP RIB
6. PRIME FORE RIB
7. SIRLOIN
8. RUMP
9. AITCHBONE
10. TOPSIDE AND SILVERSIDE
11. THICK FLANK
12. THIN FLANK
13. BRISKET
14. CLOD
15. SHIN 16. LEG

Guide to Buying and Cooking Meat

Beef

Use for	British cuts	Cooking time	Accompaniments
Roasting	Sirloin on or off bone (Sirloin as joint) Ribs (Rolled ribs, Fillet (Topside, blade) Aitchbone (good quality) Topside Rump Leg of mutton cut*	15 minutes per lb. plus 15 minutes over. Well-done. 20 minutes per lb. plus 20 minutes over or 40 minutes per lb. in very slow oven, see page 22	Yorkshire pudding Mustard Horseradish sauce Roast potatoes Thin gravy
Grilling and Frying	Rump steak (T-bone) Fillet (Topside) Sirloin (Porterhouse) Entrecôte	5–15 minutes depending on thickness and personal preference, see pages 45 and 54	Chipped or mashed potatoes Salad Tomatoes Mushrooms
Stewing or Braising	Skirt (Topside or round) Blade bone and chuck Leg of mutton cut Brisket Flank	1½–3 hours, see also under Pressure Cooking, pages 58 and 65	Mixed vegetables Dumplings Thickened gravy
Pickling or Boiling	Brisket Shin or leg Silverside Flank Aitchbone	1½–3 hours, see page 70	Vegetables or salad
Stock for Soup	Neck Shin or leg Clod Marrow bone Oxtail Flank	1½–3 hours, see page 17	

*This is a piece cut from the shoulder and is best roasted very slowly, see page 23 under Beef.

Note: If you are doubtful about tenderness of any cuts of meat for roasting, roast slowly as instructed on page 23 under Beef.

Lamb or Mutton

Use for	British cuts	Cooking time	Accompaniments
Roasting	Leg Loin and saddle Best end of neck (lamb) Shoulder Breast, stuffed and rolled	20 minutes per lb. plus 20 minutes over, see page 24	Mutton: redcurrant jelly Lamb: mint jelly or mint sauce Fresh peas
Grilling and Frying	Loin chops (Shoulder) Gigot chops (Chump chops) Cutlets (Best end of neck or rib chops) (use as part of mixed grill)	10–15 minutes see pages 48 and 55	Chipped potatoes Tomatoes Mushrooms Peas Salads
Stewing, Braising or Boiling	Neck (Shank) Breast Leg Shoulder	1½–2½ hours, see pages 59, 67 and 71	Mixed vegetables Creamed potatoes
Soups or Stock	Scrag end of neck Head Trotters	1½–2½ hours, see page 17	
Pickling or Boiling	Breast Leg Shoulder	1½–2 hours, see page 71	Potatoes Mixed vegetables

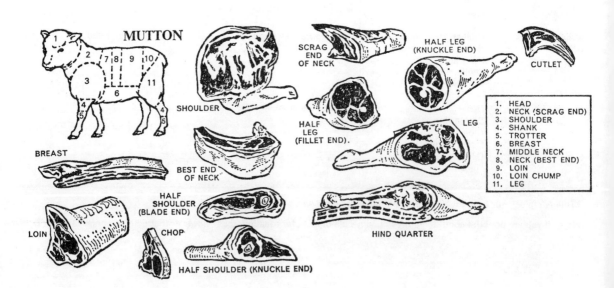

MUTTON

SHOULDER

BREAST

LOIN

HALF SHOULDER (BLADE END)

CHOP

HALF SHOULDER (KNUCKLE END)

BEST END OF NECK

SCRAG END OF NECK

HALF LEG (FILLET END).

HALF LEG (KNUCKLE END)

LEG

HIND QUARTER

CUTLET

1. HEAD
2. NECK (SCRAG END)
3. SHOULDER
4. SHANK
5. TROTTER
6. BREAST
7. MIDDLE NECK
8. NECK (BEST END)
9. LOIN
10. LOIN CHUMP
11. LEG

Veal

Use for	British cuts	Cooking time	Accompaniments
Roasting	Shoulder (Leg) Breast Best end of neck Loin Fillet Chump end of loin	30 minutes per lb. plus 30 minutes over, see page 27	Sausages Veal stuffing or other well-flavoured stuffing – keep well basted Bacon rolls
Grilling or Frying	Chops from loin (Cutlets) Best end of neck chops Thin slices from leg (fillets) to make escalopes when cooked	15–20 minutes, see pages 49 and 55	Chipped potatoes Tomatoes Mushrooms Slices of lemon
Stewing or Braising	Breast Fillet Knuckle Middle or scrag end of neck	1½–3 hours, see pages 69 and 56	Mixed vegetables Various sauces
Boiling	Head Feet Breast	1½–2½ hours, see page 71	Mixed vegetables Salads
Stock for Soup	Feet Knuckle	1½–2½ hours, see page 17	

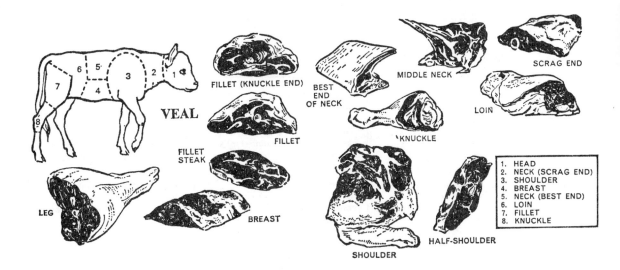

VEAL

FILLET (KNUCKLE END)
BEST END OF NECK
MIDDLE NECK
SCRAG END
FILLET
LOIN
FILLET STEAK
KNUCKLE
LEG
BREAST
SHOULDER
HALF-SHOULDER

1. HEAD
2. NECK (SCRAG END)
3. SHOULDER
4. BREAST
5. NECK (BEST END)
6. LOIN
7. FILLET
8. KNUCKLE

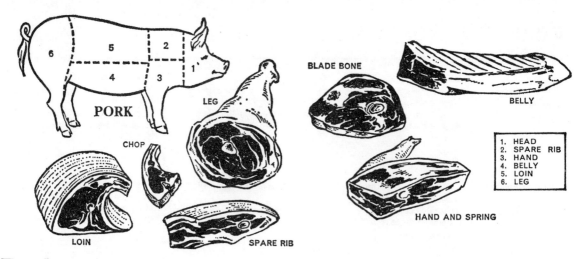

PORK

1. HEAD
2. SPARE RIB
3. HAND
4. BELLY
5. LOIN
6. LEG

LOIN   CHOP   LEG   SPARE RIB   BLADE BONE   BELLY   HAND AND SPRING

Pork

Use for	British cuts	Cooking time	Accompaniments
Roasting	Loin (Cushion) Leg Blade bone Spare rib	30 minutes per lb. plus 30 minutes over, see page 29	Sage and onion stuffing Mustard Apple sauce Orange salad
Grilling or Frying	Chops from loin (rib chops) Chump chops Spare rib chops	15–20 minutes, see pages 56 and 50	Apple sauce Apple rings Sage and onion stuffing Tomatoes Mushrooms
Boiling or Stewing	Head Hand and spring Belly Cuts given for roasting	2¼ hours, see pages 63 and 71	Salads Mixed vegetables

Bacon and Ham

Use for	British cuts	Cooking time	Accompaniments
Roasting or Baking	Gammon slipper (Ham leg) Middle gammon Back and ribs Joint top streaky	20 minutes per lb. and 20 minutes over. If well done cook like pork for 25 minutes per lb., see page 31	Mustard Salads Unusual garnishes such as baked apples, oranges, pineapple
Grilling or Frying	Top streaky (Middle cut) Prime streaky (Streaky bacon) Thin streaky Gammon slipper Middle gammon Corner gammon Long back Short back Back and ribs Top Prime collar	Few minutes only for thin rashers but with thick slices of gammon cook outside fairly quickly, then reduce heat to cook through to the middle. Keep gammon or rashers well brushed with fat when grilling, see pages 52 and 56	Eggs, tomatoes, mushrooms, etc., for breakfast Vegetables or salads for main meals

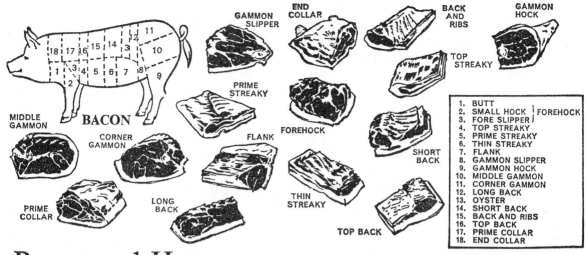

			1. BUTT
			2. SMALL HOCK ⎫ FOREHOCK
			3. FORE SLIPPER ⎭
			4. TOP STREAKY
			5. PRIME STREAKY
			6. THIN STREAKY
			7. FLANK
			8. GAMMON SLIPPER
			9. GAMMON HOCK
			10. MIDDLE GAMMON
			11. CORNER GAMMON
			12. LONG BACK
			13. OYSTER
			14. SHORT BACK
			15. BACK AND RIBS
			16. TOP BACK
			17. PRIME COLLAR
			18. END COLLAR

Bacon and Ham

Boiling or Braising	Forehock (Cushion) Prime streaky (Shoulder) Flank back (Picnic ham) Gammon slipper Gammon hock Middle gammon Corner gammon Long back Back and ribs Top back Prime collar End of collar Oyster cut	Soak well if you want very mild flavour, then simmer gently for 20–45 minutes per lb. and 20–45* minutes over. Do not boil too quickly. A pressure cooker can be used, see pages 61 and 72. Ham or bacon stock is excellent for soups.	Any vegetables – beans and peas are particularly good with boiled bacon Salads

*The apparent discrepancy in boiling times depends a great deal on the cut of bacon. The more expensive gammon will cook quicker than cheaper cuts. Often the bacon, when covered with liquid is such a tight fit in the pan that to prevent the liquid boiling over you cannot boil too quickly. This does not matter, the slow cooking will keep it beautifully tender, but it does mean that you must use a longer cooking period.

Various Methods of Cooking Meat

As you will see from the charts on the preceding pages it is important to choose the appropriate cut of meat for the method of cooking to be used. Below are a few general rules to remember when cooking meat. You will find detailed instructions for cooking beef, lamb, veal, pork, bacon and ham on pages 7–11.

Roasting

1 Remember if you add too much fat when roasting meat it hardens the outside.
2 Too little fat on a lean joint will make it dry.

Grilling

1 As grilling is a very quick process you must choose really first-quality meat.
2 Make certain that your grill is really hot before you start cooking.
3 Seal the outside as quickly as possible so that the flavour is retained and meat keeps moist.
4 Because grilling is done under a really high heat, keep meat well brushed with oil, fat or butter.

Frying

1 The same rules about quality apply as for grilling.
2 It is better to use shallow fat for meat rather than deep fat.
3 Seal the outside of the meat by putting into hot fat.
4 Fry on both sides as directed in the recipes,

then lower heat to make sure the meat is cooked through to the middle.

Stewing, casseroling, braising, boiling

1 The important thing is to realise that you are dealing with less tender pieces of meat and in consequence need to cook slowly.
2 Do not try to hurry the cooking, for you will only make the meat very tough.
3 The difference between braising and stewing is that meat is actually cooked in a thickened liquid when it is braised.
4 You will see a further definition of the term boiling on page 69. As stressed there, boiling is a misnomer, in that you never boil meat rapidly, you allow it to simmer gently.
5 On the whole, you cannot harm boiled meat by giving it a little longer than stated.

Terms Used in Meat Cookery

Basting
This is spooning fat over the meat as it cooks. The object is to help it keep moist and brown. It is unnecessary when you are using a covered roaster or when wrapping in foil.

Blanching
To treat food with boiling water. Certain meats, in particular tripe and sweetbreads, are blanched to improve the colour. You simply put them in a pan with water, bring to the boil, then throw away the water. The meat is then ready to cook in the normal fashion.

Chining
This is cutting the bones away from the meat. The purpose here is to make the meat easier to carve.

Marinating
This is soaking meat, generally in oil and vinegar, to give both flavour and to make it tender. It is particularly useful before cooking steak. Blend equal quantities of oil and vinegar or wine together. You can add seasoning to taste and a few drops of Worcestershire or Tabasco sauce. Make up enough to give about ¼ inch at the bottom of a dish. Put the meat in this and allow it to stand. After an hour turn it over and let the other side absorb the marinade. Leave a minimum of 2–3 hours, if possible.

Scoring
This is making shallow cuts in the surface of meat or its fat to improve its appearance or facilitate carving as with pork crackling. The fat of ham is generally scored after cooking when the skin has been removed. It is done in a definite pattern, usually a diamond shape.

Sealing
Sealing the outer surface of meat is a very important stage in cooking it. That is why you are told to roast meat in a hot oven, to put meat under a hot grill or into hot fat. By doing this you seal in the flavour, so keeping the flesh as moist and succulent as possible.

Skimming
Very often when boiling meats a certain greyish scum appears on the top. This is quite harmless, but in order to keep the meat looking attractive it is important to remove this. Simply take from the top of the liquid with a metal spoon.

Sliver
This is a cookery term which means cutting into very small slices. It is generally used to describe something like garlic where you must cut very thin or small portions.

Tenderizing
This is a method used to ensure that meat will not be tough. Steaks are often tenderized by beating with a rolling pin or a special meat tenderizer. The object is to break down the fibres in the meat, to allow the heat and the butter or fat used to baste to penetrate, giving a better texture and taste. A marinade, see opposite, is a form of tenderizing and so, of course, is the method chosen for cooking the meat.

To bone meat before cooking
Many people find meat difficult to carve. It is possible to have leg, shoulder, sirloin and breast of lamb boned before cooking to enable the joints to be stuffed easily, if this is required, and to simplify carving when cooked. If the butcher has not boned the meat it is not parti-

cularly difficult to bone yourself. You need a sharp, firm knife, not a carving knife but a good kitchen knife. Cut the meat down as near the bone as possible. When you feel the blade of the knife touch the bone, start to work very slowly and cut round the bone, gently moving the meat away with your other hand. If you do this slowly you will not waste the meat.

To Add Interest in Meat Cookery

Capers
Used to flavour a sauce traditionally served with boiled mutton or lamb, also to add to rather dull casseroles where you need a sharp flavour.

Chilli sauce
A hot pungent sauce to use to make spicy casseroles.

Gherkins
These give a bite to meat salads.

Mustard
English and French mustards should always be kept available, not only to serve as a condiment with meat but to add to meat in cooking. To make up English mustard blend it with water to a thick paste. It does keep better if blended with a little milk or even with two or three drops of vinegar added to the water.

Pickled walnuts, pickled onions, piccalilli, chutneys
These can be added to casseroles in varying quantities. Serve with meat dishes or with salads containing meat.

Soy or soya sauce
Used to add flavour and seasoning to Chinese-type meat dishes.

Tabasco sauce
Used to add a really strong, hot flavour to an otherwise flavourless meat casserole.

Tomato flavourings
Canned tomatoes are excellent in meat cookery, choose the plum-shaped if possible.
Concentrated tomato paste or purée in tins or tubes.
Ketchup is less potent than purée.

Vinegar
Brown malt vinegar is the most generally used in meat cookery. A red, wine vinegar is often used for French dressing to serve with meat.

Worcestershire sauce
A dash added to an ordinary casserole dish brings out the flavour and gives a bite. Many people like this served with steaks.

Fruit in meat cookery

Fruit and fruit juices do a great deal to make meat dishes interesting.

Beef
Because it is a strong flavoured meat you need fruit with bite and flavour. Apples and prunes blend well.

Lamb or mutton
Apples (as apple purée), apricots, peaches, redcurrants in the form of redcurrant jelly, cranberries in the form of cranberry jelly, gooseberry jelly because it is sharp, gives a good flavour to lamb.

Veal
This does not have a pronounced flavour, so apple sauce goes well with veal, particularly if the sauce has the bite of lemon juice added. Lemon juice or lemon rind used in stuffings is the ideal accompaniment to veal as it seems to bring out the rather delicate flavour.

Pork, ham or bacon
Most fruits blend well with pork, etc., particularly apples, oranges, pineapple, peaches and pears.

Herbs to use in meat cookery

The judicious use of herbs in meat cookery gives individual and very delicious flavourings.

The following may be taken as a guide, but obviously part of the enjoyment of cooking is to experiment and you will be able to try variations on those given.

Balm

This has a slight lemon flavour and it is excellent in stuffing, in place of parsley, as well as with parsley. It is particularly good with delicate-flavoured meat like veal, and in salads.

Basil

This has a mild clove flavour and is not unlike a bay leaf, and can be used in exactly the same way.

Bay leaf

Excellent in meat casseroles, stews or even added to a meat sauce or gravy. Lift out before serving. You can buy bay leaves ready dried and the flavour is still fairly strong. Keep the dried leaves in air-tight jars.

Borage

This has a very faint cucumber taste and a little chopped borage leaf adds a great deal of interest to a green salad.

Celery

Celery seed can be put into most casseroles when fresh celery is unavailable.

Chervil

Leaves which are not unlike parsley, with an aroma of aniseed. Can be chopped and used in place of parsley in stuffings, particularly for lamb, or in a stew or casserole.

Chives

One of the most usual herbs in every type of cookery and it should not be neglected in meat cookery. If the stronger flavour of onion is not liked then the delicate chopped chives could be substituted in many savoury meat dishes. Add a little to veal to give slightly more bite. Use it in salads of various kinds.

Dill

It is a great pity that this herb is so rarely available in this country. While it is a better herb to use with fish, it is also excellent in a salad dressing to serve with meat.

Garlic

This is invaluable in so many savoury meat dishes. It must be remembered that garlic is very strong and unless you are sure that everyone in the household will enjoy it be sparing when using garlic. Take just one clove, skin it, and for the most delicate flavour in a salad, sauce or stew, cut the clove and rub it round the salad bowl or the saucepan. For a more definite flavour, crush the clove and add to the other ingredients. If fried onions are used in the same recipe fry the garlic with them.

Horseradish

Although basically it is a vegetable, the grated root has a hot flavour and is used for a sauce to serve with beef. A little can be added to casseroles to give a more interesting flavour.

Marjoram

One of the best herbs to use when cooking lamb. Chop fresh marjoram very finely and halfway through roasting lamb sprinkle with the herb. A little can be put into a casserole made with lamb or mutton. A pinch can be added to the mayonnaise or French dressing to serve with cold lamb or mutton.

Mint

Many people consider that lamb is incomplete without mint sauce. If you are growing mint remember there are various kinds, each one giving a slightly different flavour. For example, the spearmint which is the most usual kind has a different taste to the peppermint. Either are equally good in a mint sauce. When the fresh mint is not obtainable you can buy ready dried mint, dry your own or make a very excellent mint jelly.

Oregano

This Italian herb is generally obtained dried in this country and is really a wild marjoram. It is excellent in pasta dishes.

Parsley

It is probably one of the most useful of all

garnishes. It is essential to add to many stuffings and casserole dishes.

Pennyroyal
This is a type of strong mint and could be used in place of mint.

Rosemary
Although rosemary is used more often with poultry, it is an excellent herb for veal. When roasting veal or lamb just sprinkle a little chopped rosemary over the joint. Add a small amount to stuffings to serve with these meats. Put a pinch into a salad or salad dressing.

Sage
Sage is the herb mostly associated with pork in sage and onion stuffing. It has a very strong flavour and should be used carefully when mixing with other herbs. A little sage could be added to most casserole dishes, but care should be taken, particularly with dried sage, that it is not used too lavishly.

Saffron
This comes from a flower and a pinch of powdered saffron, or a few strands of saffron, can be added to casseroles. In order to get the very best flavour from saffron buy the yellow strands. Let them dissolve in cold water for a while and then put into a casserole.

Savory
A herb not unlike thyme. Use in stuffings.

Sorrel
The leaves of sorrel are rather acid and they are rather biting to put into salads or stews unless used very carefully.

Tansy
This is a very old-fashioned herb rarely obtained now, which is a pity because a little of the chopped leaves can be added to salad dressings, salads or put into a casserole.

Tarragon
A few leaves of tarragon, finely chopped, are excellent in a salad. Do not add too many as the flavour is very strong. They are also excellent infused in vinegar so that the vinegar absorbs their flavour.

Thyme
Thyme is probably, after parsley, one of the most useful of all herbs. It is put into stuffings and added to casseroles. You can get both ordinary and lemon thyme; these have slightly different flavours.

To preserve mint in sugar
1 Chop the mint finely and put a layer into a jar.
2 Add an equal layer of sugar.
3 Continue in this way until the jar is full.
4 Seal down.

Mint jelly
1 Make a syrup with 8 oz. sugar and $\frac{1}{2}$ pint water.
2 Add $\frac{1}{4}$ pint vinegar and $1\frac{1}{2}$ dessertspoons powdered gelatine.
3 Stir in 2–3 tablespoons chopped mint.
4 Pour into jars and seal down.
5 Store in a cool place.

Spices to use in meat cookery

Allspice (mixed spice)
This is used in stews and casseroles.

Caraway
One normally uses just the dried seeds of caraway and about a teaspoon could be added to a meat stew or casserole to give an unusual flavour. They are best used in a casserole containing a fairly high amount of onion.

Cayenne pepper
This is the hot spicy pepper. Excellent added to certain casseroles.

Celery salt
When celery is out of season, celery salt or celery seed (see herbs, page 13) add an excellent flavour. The latter must, of course, be strained.

Chilli powder
This is used in various savoury meat dishes, in particular Chilli con carne, which comes from Mexico. A little could be added to home-made curry if wished.

It must be realised that chilli is unbearably hot for many people, and unless you have a taste for dishes containing this, do cut down the quantity very drastically.

Cinnamon
This is used for rather savoury meat stews and casseroles.

Cloves
Add to ham when glazing.

Coriander and cumin
The seeds can be added to meat curries to give a really good flavour.

Curry powder or curry paste
This is the basis for curries.

Ginger
This adds a little more flavour to a curry or hot sauce.

Mace
This is excellent added to many casseroles. Use sparingly.

Nutmeg
This is excellent added to many casseroles. Use sparingly.

Paprika
This is used for the sweeter goulash.

Pepper
White is for table use; black pepper should be used for meat cookery or better still, keep peppercorns and grind them yourself, in a pepper mill, when needed.

Peppercorns
In many meat casseroles you can actually put the peppercorns into the dish, or the sauce, and strain afterwards.

Turmeric
This is generally used in pickles but is also excellent added to a curry or savoury dishes. It also adds colour.

Vegetables in meat cookery

Naturally, vegetables will be served throughout the year with meat, but in meat casseroles certain vegetables add a great deal of flavour.

Artichokes – with beef or lamb.
Asparagus – with veal, steak or ham.
Aubergines – with lamb, mutton or pork.
Beans of all kinds – with most meats.
Celery, celeriac, etc. – with most meats.
Chestnuts – with veal or lamb.
Corn on the cob – with pork or ham.
Cucumber, raw or pickled – with cold beef in particular.
They blend well with all meats.
Leeks – with lamb or mutton.
Mushrooms – with all meats.
Onions – with all meats.
Peppers, red or green (capsicums) – excellent blended with most meats but particularly good with lamb, mutton, pork or veal.
Peppers (the hot red chilli pepper) – best with strong flavoured meats like beef or mutton.
Sauerkraut (fermented cabbage) – particularly good with pork, sausages or ham.
Spinach – excellent with all meats.
Tomatoes – excellent with all meats.
Vegetables such as cabbage, carrots, sprouts and cauliflower, etc., not given above, blend with every type of meat.

To make a purée of vegetables

Simply cook the vegetables in the normal way, then mash or rub through a sieve and reheat with a knob of butter or margarine and plenty of seasoning.

Wines used in meat cookery

You will find wine used in a number of recipes in this book. When you are making a savoury dish or casserole you can substitute a certain amount of wine for the stock or water.

Beef, which has a strong flavour, is best cooked with a red Burgundy or Bordeaux.
Lamb and mutton can be cooked with a red wine, a vin rosé or a fairly dry white wine.
Veal needs a white wine rather than a red, so that its delicate flavour is not spoiled.

Pork, though less used in casserole dishes, can be cooked with either red or white wine or with cider.

Ham or gammon is often improved by adding cider, a dry white wine or even ginger ale or fruit juices.

To stuff joints for roasting

Recipes for various stuffings are given. Here are various suggestions for inserting in the joint.

1 Breast of meat, i.e. lamb, veal, etc. Bone, or ask the butcher to remove the bone, from the breast. Then spread with the stuffing, roll firmly and tie.
2 Loin. Cut down the meat the way of the bones, so making a pocket. Insert the stuffing and tie firmly. You may prefer to cook the stuffing in a separate container in the oven.
3 Shoulder or leg. This can either be boned, see method for boning meat page 12, or you can make a deep slit down the meat so forming a pocket and put the stuffing in here.
4 Flat joints such as topside of beef, large fillet of veal, etc. Cut the meat through the centre two-thirds of the way across, so forming a large pocket. Insert the stuffing, and skewer or tie.

To use minced beef

Throughout this book you will find many recipes using minced beef and care must be taken that it is not over-cooked otherwise it has a tendency to become very dry.

To Make Bone Stock

Many recipes for sauces, gravy and casserole dishes require stock. This is not difficult to make and it cannot be disputed that in many dishes a good stock will improve the flavour. It is, however, considered quite dangerous to keep stock for a great length of time, unless stored in a refrigerator.

Make the stock as freshly as possible; a pressure cooker enables you to do this quickly and easily, and instructions for this method are given opposite. The traditional method of making stock in a saucepan is as follows:

cooking time: 3–4 hours

you will need:

2 lb. bones – large marrow bones if possible	1 bay leaf salt and pepper cold water to cover

1 Cover bones of beef (for brown stock), of veal or poultry (for white stock), with water.
2 Add bay leaf, salt and pepper.
3 Simmer gently for several hours.
4 Vegetables can be added, if wished, but they cause the stock to spoil more rapidly.
5 Strain stock.
6 When cold lift off any fat from the top.
7 If stock has been kept for several days, even in a refrigerator, boil well before use.

To make stock in a pressure cooker

cooking time: 45 minutes

you will need:
ingredients as for bone stock

1 Put all the ingredients into a pressure cooker, prepared as opposite, but using 2 pints water only.
2 Fix the lid and bring steadily to 15 lb. pressure.
3 Reduce the heat and cook for 45 minutes.
4 Allow pressure to return to normal before removing lid.
5 Strain, cool as opposite.

To make stock quickly

If you use the recipes given for making stock in a saucepan or pressure cooker it is important to stand the stock in a cool place and bring it to the boil daily. This is a chore for a person with little time.

Make use of the excellent meat or yeast extracts or beef and chicken bouillon cubes available, for these give you good-flavoured stocks within a minute.

Gravy

To serve gravy with roast meat

It is correct to serve a thick gravy with stuffed meat and a thin one with unstuffed meat. Obviously, this rule will be followed according to personal taste. If you like a thickened gravy then this is the one to serve for your family.

When serving underdone beef many people prefer to use just the juice that flows as the meat is carved. This is not possible with other meats which have a longer cooking time and therefore should not have juice flowing when they are carved. Instructions for making gravy are given below.

To make gravy
Thin gravy

1 Pour away practically all the fat from the roasting tin, leaving the residue of the meat to give flavour.
2 Add about 1 teaspoon flour and approximately ½ pint stock, or water flavoured with meat or vegetable extract, or a bouillon cube.
3 Bring to the boil. Cook until clear and strain.

Thickened gravy

1 Leave about 1 tablespoon fat in the meat tin.
2 Add approximately 1 oz. flour.
3 Cook for several minutes together.
4 Add just over ½ pint stock, or water flavoured with meat or vegetable extract, or a bouillon cube.
5 Bring to the boil, cook until thick and strain.

To serve gravy with fried or grilled meat

Although it is not usual, some people like gravy with meat that is fried or grilled. The method would be exactly the same as a gravy for roast meat. The surplus fat could be tipped from the frying pan and the gravy made in this. You must stir very gently and carefully to avoid sticking as the gravy thickens.

Obviously you will not wish to put the grill pan over the heat on top of the cooker, so simply tip some of the fat that has dripped from the meat while grilling into a saucepan, and make the gravy in this.

To vary the flavour of gravy

The preceding recipes give the basic way to make gravy, but obviously you will not always wish it to taste the same. Here are some quick ways to vary the flavour.

1 **Add tomato purée.** Use 1 dessertspoon or 1 tablespoon to ½ pint gravy, or purée made from fresh or canned tomatoes or even a very little tomato ketchup.
2 **Add various herbs,** see page 13.
3 Fry a little finely **chopped onion** in the fat before adding the rest of the ingredients.
4 Add a few drops of **Worcestershire, chilli** or **Tabasco sauce.**

Carving

Good carving not only makes a joint of meat go further but it produces a more appetising-looking portion. It is important to remember:
1 Use a really well-sharpened knife. Buy a steel so that you can sharpen the knife each time before using. If you have a very large family it is a good idea to use a second knife if possible, the heat of the meat will blunt a carving knife.
2 Take care to choose a carving knife that feels comfortable to hold.
3 Most joints are better carved with a knife that has a fairly firm rigid blade, but ham can be carved with a lighter more flexible blade.
4 Make absolutely certain you use a proper carving fork with a guard to prevent the hand from being cut should the knife slip.

To carve beef

Carve this in large slices *across* the joint. When sirloin of beef is cooked on the bone you should first remove the backbone or chine, then cut the first slices along the bone. Next turn the joint and cut slices at right angles from the bone.

To carve lamb or mutton

Cut thickish slices *downwards*, but certain joints are best carved in the following way:

Saddle

Cut very long slices, first across the centre of the joint, then cutting downwards. Next cut slanting slices from the remainder of the joint.

Shoulder

Follow the contour of the bone, cutting slices round it. If the end of the shoulder is held in a napkin it gives a firmer grip.

To carve veal

Leg or shoulder

Carve downwards or round the bone.

Loin

Cut downwards into chops.

Fillet

Carve across the meat.

To carve pork

Shoulder or leg

Follow the contour of the bone, cutting slices round it.

Loin

This is easy to cut, since the skin is scored before cooking to give a good crackling, and the butcher generally saws through the bones. Cut slices downwards.

Dripping

This is fat that melts and runs from meat when it is roasted. In these days of small joints you will, of course, have very little fat left in the tin after cooking, but do not waste it, particularly dripping that comes from beef – it has a first-class flavour; use in all types of cooking.

Most butchers will sell a really well-clarified dripping. Do not attempt to store the dripping from the meat for any length of time unless it has been well clarified, see opposite.

To use dripping

Dripping, when clarified, can be used in all forms of cooking. In the old days it was used for pastry, even for cakes, and certainly for roasting potatoes and frying. Nowadays most people use cooking fat or margarine, but undoubtedly the flavour of good dripping is unbeatable in meat dishes, i.e. for stews, roasting and for roasting potatoes. Where the recipe says 'put fat over the meat', then a well-clarified meat dripping is ideal.

Naturally it is better to put a beef dripping on beef, lamb on lamb, etc.

To clarify dripping

cooking time: 5–10 minutes

1 Cover the dripping with cold water in a deep saucepan.
2 Bring to the boil.
3 Allow fat and water to cool.
4 You will then be able to lift off the fat, leaving most of the impurities in the water.
5 You will find that when you turn the piece of fat over there may be one or two tiny little pieces of meat or jelly still clinging to the underside of the fat. Scrape these off.

To render down fat

Mention is made of the dripping that comes from meat when roasting, but sometimes when you are preparing a casserole or a stew you will find rather a lot of fat which you may not wish to use in that particular dish. It is econo-mical if you render this down to give a really first-class dripping.

Put the pieces of fat into a tin and heat very slowly in the oven until you are left with dry, brown, shrivelled skin and a good amount of fat in the tin. Then treat this like dripping, clarifying it in the same way.

To Roast Meat

Roasting meat is probably one of the most popular methods of cooking it, particularly where you are sure of a good-quality meat. You will find suggestions for both quick and slow roasting. The reason for choosing slow roasting is to tenderise frozen and cheaper cuts of meat, but it has another advantage: if you are going out and wish to leave the meat cooking for some time, without attention, the slow method may be more practical.

Some people consider that there is less shrink-age with the slow method of roasting.

Follow the directions in the various tables, see pages 7–11, but at all times you are the perfect judge of timing, since your oven temperature may vary slightly from the average. The posi-tion in which you place the meat in the oven has a bearing on the cooking time. If you put it in the hottest part of the oven, the top, you will cook in a shorter period of time than if it were placed in the middle of an electric, or lower down in a gas oven. You will find that electric cookers with top and bottom elements or bottom elements only are also hot at the bottom of the oven. Check this with the manufacturer's booklet that comes with your cooker. This will tell you the correct position for fast and slow roasting in your particular cooker.

You will find below some of the mistakes that can be made when roasting meat, with sug-gestions as to how they can be overcome.

1 Tough meat. This can be due to:
(a) using frozen meat that has not defrosted properly.
(b) roasting cheap cuts of meat too quickly.
(c) over-cooking, which toughens meat far more than people realise.
2 Over-cooked meat. If you have followed the usual timing, but the joint was, perhaps, rather broad and yet thin, you could have cooked it for 10–15 minutes less. Once meat has started to cook, these extra minutes make a lot of difference in achieving perfection.

3 Dry and unappetising meat. If the meat was particularly lean it needed extra fat spread over before cooking and some basting during cooking.

4 Flavourless meat. If the meat has been deep frozen it is inclined to lose a little of its flavour, and that is where slow cooking and the judicious use of herbs and stuffings helps enormously.

5 Under-cooked meat. See point 2 on overcook-ing.

6 Hard outside to meat. This is generally due to excessive cooking, too great a heat, or using too much fat. People are very inclined to put an enormous amount of dripping or other fat on to the meat, and this makes a very hard coating, as when meat is fried. If you do not like this hard crispy outside, then use a covered roaster, foil or the minimum of fat.

7 Badly shrunken meat. Frozen meat tends to shrink more than fresh. Meat that has been cooked too quickly shrinks more than meat cooked steadily.

Spit roasting

In the old days, in large kitchens, meat was cooked over a turning spit. This fashion has now returned to a degree, with spits in ovens or under the grills of gas and electric cookers.

The great advantage is that the meat turns during cooking, and you do get an even coating on the outside. The same rules apply about brushing with fat. Very lean meat should be basted once or twice during cooking. Fatter meat can be cooked without attention.

Cooking times for roasting meat

It is virtually impossible to give the time to the minute. The tables on pages 7 to 11 help you by giving the orthodox time at the average temperature. So often ovens vary, and you must check with your cooker manufacturer's instruction book or card to make sure you have the right oven temperature.

If you are using stuffing you must add the weight of the stuffing to the meat, i.e. if the joint weighs 5 lb. without stuffing, but 6 lb. by the time you have put in the stuffing, you work on a 6 lb. joint.

To roast meat in a covered roaster

In order to keep the oven clean a covered roasting tin is often used. Do not imagine that this will give you the effect of steamed meat. If you make certain that the top of the joint is at least an inch below the top of the tin, you get automatic basting as the fat (either from the fat you add or from the meat itself) becomes heated, splutters, hits the top of the tin and drops back again on to the meat. In this way meat is brown enough for most people.

If you want a very crisp outside you can remove the lid towards the end of cooking time.

For very crisp crackling pork it is not a good idea to use a covered roaster.

Because it takes longer for the heat to reach meat in a covered roaster it is advisable to allow an extra 15 minutes cooking time.

To use foil for roasting

There are two ways of using foil.

1 Wrap the meat in a complete parcel. In this way it is kept very moist, but for many people it tends to have a slight flavour of steamed meat. You can avoid this by opening the foil and letting the meat brown towards the end of the cooking time. If using this method of cooking meat you need allow only an extra 5–10 minutes for the heat to penetrate through the piece of foil.

2 Put the meat into a meat tin and then place a piece of foil over the top to take the place of the lid of a covered roaster. The foil should not actually touch the meat. This gives the effect of a covered roaster and the meat browns. Allow about 15 minutes more cooking time.

If you do not wish to extend the cooking time use a slightly hotter oven when cooking in foil. This does not produce a scorching result, as the meat is well protected.

With lean meat it is advisable to grease foil slightly before putting round meat; this prevents the possibility of the meat sticking to the foil.

To pot roast

1 Put a little fat in the bottom of a pan, which should be a good heavy one with a well-fitting lid.

2 Brown the meat lightly, then lift it out of the pan and either insert a small trivet or rack and lift the meat on to this.

3 Put enough water in the pan to give about 1 inch depth, but make sure it does not cover the meat as you do not want it to taste stewed.

4 Season well and put on the lid.

5 Allow approximately 40 minutes to the lb., add vegetables during the cooking period so they get tender at same time as the meat.

6 When you dish up you will find the liquid at the bottom makes a delicious gravy.

7 If by any chance you do not have a trivet then lift the meat on to a bed of vegetables, but you must of course, keep these in very big pieces so that they are not over-cooked by the time the meat is ready.

To pot roast in a pressure cooker

A pressure cooker can be used for pot roasting. Any meat that can be roasted in the normal way is suitable, and if by chance you have a less tender piece of meat, then try pot roasting.

1 Heat a little fat at the bottom of the cooker.

2 Brown the meat well in the fat, then lift the meat out of the cooker, insert the trivet and replace meat.

3 Add water, allow ½ pint for a joint that takes

up to 15 minutes' pressure cooking time, and add an additional ¼ pint water for each 15 minutes over. For example, for a joint taking 45 minutes you need 1 pint water.

4 Beef needs 10 minutes per lb. at 15 lb. pressure. Lamb, veal, pork need 12 minutes per lb. Roasting chicken needs 5 minutes per lb.

5 Allow pressure to drop at room temperature. You will find the liquid in the cooker makes excellent gravy.

6 If wished the pressure can be allowed to drop and vegetables put in at the right time to allow them to cook. The meat and vegetables are then ready together.

To add seasoning when roasting

Some people feel that too much salt put on meat before it is roasted tends to make it slightly tough. Other people feel that the outside of a joint should be seasoned. This is a matter of personal taste. If you are sprinkling salt and pepper over the joint do it carefully.

To roast potatoes

If roasting round joint you need about 2 oz. fat to each 1 lb. potatoes.

1 Peel and dry potatoes.

2 Roll in hot fat in tin, using two tablespoons to turn potatoes round in fat, and allow approximately 50–60 minutes' cooking time. If preferred the potatoes may be cooked in fat in a separate tin from the meat.

3 Another method is to cook for 5–10 minutes in boiling salted water first, drain well, then roast. This produces potatoes that are floury on the inside yet crisp outside.

4 When cooked, drain with perforated spoon before serving.

To roast new potatoes

It is surprising how rarely new potatoes are roasted, and they are absolutely delicious. Simply wash, dry, but do not skin potatoes, and continue as roast potatoes, allowing approximately 45 minutes when they are small.

To roast parsnips or swedes

Parsnips or swedes can be roasted in exactly the same way as potatoes; if the parsnips are very large, halve or even quarter them, or cut the swedes into similar sized pieces. You may find, however, that they will be slightly 'woody' unless they are boiled beforehand. Put the peeled parsnips or swedes into boiling salted water, cook steadily for a good 10–15 minutes, depending on size. Strain carefully, and continue as for roast potatoes.

To roast onions

Medium-sized onions will take about 1¼ hours to roast. It should not be necessary to boil them first. Just roll them round well in the hot fat, and continue as roast potatoes.

Sausages

These can be baked or roasted in the oven, and if you are roasting potatoes it is quite a good idea to put the sausages in just after the potatoes have begun to cook. They need no extra fat and will be ready at the same time as the potatoes. Prick before cooking.

To roast prime cuts of beef

For the cooking times, see the table on page 7. If the family likes a very lean joint choose topside or rump or fillet. For a prime quality with a good distribution of lean and fat choose ribs of beef (for a large joint) or sirloin. Aitchbone of first-rate quality can be roasted, but is best roasted slowly. If you like a crisp outside to the meat then DO NOT use a covered roasting tin; instead put a little well-clarified dripping, see page 19, or fat on the meat, which can be seasoned lightly if liked. Either put meat in roasting tin or on trivet (rack) in the tin, or cook it on a turning spit.

1 Put meat into a hot oven (425–450°F. – Gas Mark 6–7).

2 For joints under 4 lb. the heat need not be lowered a great deal; follow times given on page 7, or in individual recipes.

3 For larger joints lower heat after first 1–1¼

hours to moderate (375°F. – Gas Mark 4) or very moderate (350°F. – Gas Mark 3) allowing longer cooking time.

Note

This information assumes that you have bought really good-quality meat. If you have bought frozen imported meat which can sometimes be tougher, although you may have bought one of the joints mentioned, it is wiser to roast this slowly as instructions below.

To roast beef slowly

cooking time: see the table on page 7

This method is suitable for frozen pieces of meat, or the less expensive cuts like brisket, leg of mutton cut, aitch-bone and less good topside.

If there is any doubt at all as to whether the meat is of top quality it will be advisable to roast slowly rather than quickly.

To roast any meat slowly follow these times:
1 Set the oven to very slow (275°F. – Gas Mark 1).
2 Allow 1¼ hours for the first lb.
3 For each additional lb. up to 7 lb. allow an extra 25 minutes; i.e. a 4 lb. joint will take 2½ hours.

or

1 Use a very moderate oven (350°F. – Gas Mark 3) and allow 50 minutes for the first lb.
2 Each additional lb. takes a further 20 minutes.

Ovens vary a great deal, so do check that this is the temperature you would normally use for the *very* slow cooking of a casserole in your particular oven.

One point to consider when roasting beef slowly is that you will be unable to cook roast potatoes or a Yorkshire pudding at the same temperature. You could overcome this by roasting slowly as directed, taking the tin out of the oven, and increasing the heat for roast potatoes or Yorkshire pudding. When these are nearly cooked return the meat to the hot oven. This short period of hot temperature will not harm it in any way.

When the meat is taken out of the oven you must, of course, have virtually completed the recommended cooking time.

Accompaniments to beef

Recipes follow for:
Yorkshire pudding, horseradish sauce or horseradish cream.

Yorkshire pudding

Use the ingredients for pancake batter, page 52. Make the batter as this recipe, and allow to stand for a while. To give a richer batter use 2 eggs; for the lightest mixture use one-third water and two-thirds milk.

To cook the pudding

cooking time: see below

Many people like individual Yorkshire puddings, in which case grease fairly deep patty tins, or put in knob of fat the size of a pea, heat for a few minutes then pour in the batter. Cook the individual Yorkshire puddings at the top of a very hot oven for about 12 minutes, reducing heat if necessary. For a large pudding put good-sized knob of fat or dripping into Yorkshire pudding tin, heat for a few minutes at the top of a very hot oven (475°F. – Gas Mark 8), pour in the batter and cook for approximately 10–15 minutes, lower the heat slightly and cook for further 10–25 minutes, depending on size of tin. Whether cooking in large or small tins this gives a puffy type of pudding, but many people consider the flavour better if baked UNDER THE MEAT – as follows:

1 Lift meat out of the roasting tin. Pour away all dripping, except 1–2 tablespoons.
2 Make sure this is very hot, pour in the batter, return to a hot oven.
3 Either put the meat on the shelf above the Yorkshire pudding tin, or on a trivet standing on shelf above.
4 Cook for approximately 30–35 minutes for a pudding made with ½ pint liquid.
5 As the pudding cooks, juices from the meat drop in to give flavour, but you do not have such a crisp light pudding.

Horseradish sauce

Whisk about a dessertspoon vinegar and 2 tablespoons grated horseradish into ½ pint white sauce, see page 86. Add a small amount of cream and pinch of sugar. Served hot.

Horseradish cream

no cooking

you will need:

little mustard
salt
pepper
good pinch sugar
¼ pint cream

2 good tablespoons grated horseradish
1 tablespoon white vinegar

1 Mix all the seasonings with the cream and whip lightly.
2 Add the horseradish and vinegar.

Stuffed brisket

cooking time: 2 hours 20 minutes

you will need for 6–8 servings:

3 lb. joint brisket of beef

for the stuffing:

2 oz. white breadcrumbs
1 chopped onion
1 tablespoon sieved tomato
½ teaspoon made mustard

salt and pepper
1 small beaten egg

1 oz. butter or dripping

1 Spread the boned meat flat on a board.
2 Mix the stuffing ingredients together. Add the egg last because it may not all be needed, if you like a fairly firm stuffing.
3 Cover the meat with stuffing.
4 Roll up and secure with skewers and string.
5 Rub with butter.
6 Place the meat bones on top.
7 Cover and bake in a fairly hot oven (375–400°F. – Gas Mark 4–5) for 20 minutes, then reduce the heat for 2 hours.

To roast mutton or lamb

For the cooking times see the table on page 8. Lamb is a meat that should be well cooked, so do ensure that you have allowed adequate cooking time.

If you like a very succulent piece of lamb, choose shoulder or half-shoulder, leg or half-leg. The lower part of the leg is the leaner piece whereas the shoulder contains the most fat. Loin or best end of neck of lamb gives you a good distribution of fat and lean, but, of course, you do have quite an amount of bone. Breast of lamb is the most economical of all and very tender, but does contain a very high percentage of fat. You can overcome this to a degree by using a stuffing such as veal stuffing, sage and onion or sausage meat mixed with more crumbs. Saddle is a very impressive joint to choose.

Mutton is less tender than lamb and in most cases it is advisable to use the slow method of roasting as described under Beef, page 23.

1 To roast the lamb or mutton season lightly on the outside. There is no need to add any fat.
2 If using a covered roaster or covering with foil allow 15 minutes' extra time.
3 Remember, if stuffing breast of lamb, that you must count this in with the total weight.
4 If you are using a covered roaster take the lid off for the last 15 minutes to crisp the outside skin.
5 Lamb or mutton should be well cooked, so start in a really hot oven (425–450°F. – Gas Mark 6–7) and reduce heat slightly (400°F. – Gas Mark 5) after the first 30–35 minutes' cooking.
6 The dripping you get from roast mutton or lamb is not as good as that from beef and many people do not keep it since it has a very distinctive flavour and cannot be used for other purposes.
7 If roasting potatoes with mutton or lamb they can be roasted round the joint, see page 22, but the fat from this meat is a little watery and you do get a rather more crisp result if you roast the potatoes separately.

Roast lamb with garlic

1 Take one tiny piece (clove) of garlic and halve it then rub the cut surfaces over the lamb before roasting.
2 For a stronger garlic flavour make a slit in the skin of leg or shoulder or lamb and insert the clove of garlic.
3 Remove before serving the lamb.

Accompaniments to mutton or lamb

You do not serve mustard with mutton or lamb. With lamb serve mint sauce or jelly. With mutton you serve onion sauce, see below. Gravy should be thin if you have not stuffed the meat, thick if you have. See page 18.

New or roast potatoes can be served with mutton or lamb.

Mint sauce

no cooking

1 Chop mint finely.
2 Add sugar to taste, vinegar and if liked a little hot water.

Onion sauce

cooking time: 50 minutes

you will need:

3 onions	1 oz. flour
water	$\frac{1}{4}$ pint milk
1 oz. butter or margarine	salt and pepper

1 Boil the onions in water in a covered saucepan until tender. Large onions will take about 45 minutes.
2 Chop the onions when cooked and keep $\frac{1}{4}$ pint of the liquid. If possible chop them on a laminated plastic surface rather than wood, since it is very difficult to get rid of the onion smell from a wooden surface.
3 Heat the butter in a pan, stir in the flour and cook for several minutes.
4 Remove from heat and add the milk, the onion stock and seasoning. Bring to the boil.
5 Add the chopped onions and re-heat.

To roast cutlets or chops

Although cutlets and chops are generally grilled or fried, they can be roasted as well. Arrange in the meat tin, and allow approximately 35 minutes for thick chops in a hot oven (425–450°F. – Gas Mark 6–7); 20–25 minutes for small cutlets.

Mutton chops are better covered and roasted by the slow method, see page 24, and allow approximately 1$\frac{1}{4}$ hours.

Roast stuffed cutlets

cooking time: see method

you will need for 4 servings:

4–8 cutlets lamb, mutton, pork or veal depending on size)	stuffing (see page 26) little fat (optional)

1 Remove the bone and press stuffing against meat, then roll neatly to form a round.
2 Grease the tin if meat is lean, place meat in it and grease top of rounds. Roast for 20 minutes for small cutlets, or up to 30 minutes for large cutlets, in a moderate oven (400°F. Gas Mark 5–6). Pork and veal need a little longer.

Chestnut-stuffed lamb

cooking time: 1$\frac{1}{4}$ hours

you will need for 4 servings:

1 onion	3 tablespoons fine breadcrumbs
2 oz. mushrooms	
2 oz. sultanas	1 egg
4 oz. cooked, mashed chestnuts	1 large boned breast of lamb

1 Mince the onion, mushrooms and sultanas.
2 Mix with the chestnuts and breadcrumbs and bind with the beaten egg.
3 Spread the mixture over the meat, roll and tie securely.
4 Bake in a moderate oven (375°F. – Gas Mark 4).
5 To improve the flavour, cover during the cooking time.

Stuffed breast of lamb

cooking time: 1$\frac{1}{4}$ hours

you will need for 4 servings:

4 oz. pork sausage meat	1 level teaspoon salt shake pepper
4 oz. soft white breadcrumbs	3 tablespoons water or milk
1 rounded tablespoon chopped parsley	1 breast lamb, approximately
1 level teaspoon dry mustard	1$\frac{1}{2}$–1$\frac{3}{4}$ lb. in weight *after* boning
2 level teaspoons finely grated onion	little lard or dripping

1 Mix together sausage meat, breadcrumbs, parsley, mustard, onion, salt and pepper and

bind with the water or milk. If mixture seems a little dry add more liquid.

2 Spread lamb thinly with stuffing, roll up tightly and secure with string or skewers.
3 Stand in baking tin, cover joint with a little lard or dripping.
4 Bake in the centre of a moderate oven (375°F. – Gas Mark 4) for 1¼ hours.
5 Transfer to a warm dish and serve with creamed potatoes, peas, garnished with raw or fried onion rings, and onion sauce, see page 25.

Variation

With tomato – all sausage meat can be used, and blend with chopped tomato instead of milk or water.

Colonial goose

cooking time: according to weight

you will need for 6–10 servings:

1 boned shoulder lamb	1 oz. butter

for the stuffing:

4 tablespoons fresh white breadcrumbs	2 teaspoons chopped parsley
1 chopped parboiled onion	1 teaspoon thyme
salt and pepper	1 teaspoon sage
1 oz. melted butter or margarine	little chopped ham or lean bacon

1 Put all the stuffing ingredients into a basin and mix lightly together.
2 Stuff the shoulder, roll up and tie securely with fine string.
3 Stand the joint on a grid in a roasting tin and cover with a little butter or margarine.
4 Roast as table on page 8.

Variation

Raisin-stuffed shoulder – boil 4 oz. long-grain rice in stock until tender, mix with ingredients as above, omitting breadcrumbs. Add 1–2 tablespoons raisins, and 1 oz. chopped blanched almonds if wished.

Hot Windsor lamb

cooking time: according to weight

you will need for 6–10 servings:
1 shoulder lamb

for sauce:

2 oz. chopped bacon	1 pint stock
1½ oz. lard	6 tomatoes
1 onion	1 tablespoon sherry
1 carrot	salt
2 oz. flour	pepper

1 Roast the lamb, see table on page 8.
2 Toss the bacon in the melted lard, add the thinly sliced onion and carrot and cook for a few minutes without browning.
3 Take the vegetables and bacon from the pan then brown the flour in the same fat and gradually stir in the stock.
4 Replace the vegetables and bacon, add the chopped tomatoes and simmer gently for 30 minutes.
5 Strain the gravy, add the sherry and seasoning to taste, and return it to the pan.
6 Heat gently for 10 minutes and serve the sauce with the lamb.

Roast lamb with bay leaves

cooking time: about 2 hours

you will need for 6 servings:

2½ lb. shoulder of lamb	juice and rind 1 lemon
2 bay leaves	2 oz. fresh breadcrumbs
4 oz. streaky bacon rashers	1 dessertspoon chopped parsley

1 Put lamb in a roasting tin, top with bay leaves, cover with bacon and roast in a hot oven (425–450°F. – Gas Mark 6–7), for 1½ hours.
2 Sprinkle over lemon juice and breadcrumbs, add lemon rind and parsley.
3 Cook for a further 20 minutes or until golden.

Crown roast of lamb

Most butchers, given reasonable notice, will prepare a crown roast for you, but if you have to do it yourself it is not particularly difficult, although it needs quite a lot of patience. You need a minimum of 12–14 chops of lamb. You may find that the butcher will send you the loin in two pieces each of about 7–8 chops. First of all, cut or chine the bottom of the chops so that you can bend the loin. Then cut away the meat from the top of the bone rather like a cutlet. Having prepared the meat, tie into a circle or crown. As you will see from the following recipe, point 1, in order that the bones do not become charred, you can protect them with foil or cutlet frills.

Stuffed crown roast of lamb

cooking time: as total weight

you will need for 6 large or 12 small servings:
loin of lamb shaped into a crown* oil for brushing
*It will probably be 4–4½ lb.

for the stuffing:
any of the stuffings in this book

to serve:
thickened gravy

to garnish:
cutlet frills parsley

1 Protect the tip of each rib bone with foil.
2 Brush the whole of the loin with a little oil.
3 Place stuffing in the centre of the loin in the meat tin and cook as table according to weight, counting the weight of the stuffing.
4 When cooked remove foil or greaseproof paper.
5 Place the crown roast in a serving dish and keep warm while making gravy.
6 To serve, place a cutlet frill on each rib and garnish with parsley.
7 Serve the gravy separately.

Saddle of lamb

cooking time: according to weight

you will need for 10–16 servings:
1 saddle lamb, ¼ pint hot water
  approximately 8 lb. 1 tablespoon flour
4 oz. butter apples
salt and pepper mint jelly

1 Remove the skin from the joint. Take the fat and kidneys from the inside.
2 Fold the flaps underneath. Tie and skewer neatly.
3 Spread the butter over the whole surface, sprinkle with salt and pepper.

4 Put into a baking tin and pour the hot water round the joint.
5 Roast in a moderate oven (350–375°F. – Gas Mark 3–4), allowing 25–30 minutes to the lb. and 30 minutes over.
6 During the last 15 minutes of cooking, add the kidneys to the meat juices in the tin.
7 Baste the joint several times during the cooking.
8 To make the gravy, pour off almost all the fat from the tin, stir in one level tablespoon of flour, add about ½ pint liquid from any of the accompanying vegetables, and cook and stir until the gravy thickens.
9 Strain into a gravy boat.
10 Attach kidneys with cocktail sticks to joint.
11 Serve surrounded with slices of baked apple topped with mint jelly.
12 To bake apples, core but do not peel, and cut into fairly thick slices.

To roast veal

For the cooking times see the table on page 9. For roasting veal choose shoulder, breast, best end of neck, loin, fillet or chump end of loin.

1 The perfect way to roast veal is to use a larding needle (which can be bought from an ironmongers) and thin strips of fat from bacon. Insert these strips through the meat so that it is really kept moist during cooking. Otherwise wrap veal in plenty of buttered foil when cooking or cover top with 1–2 oz. fat.
2 If you have larded the meat or covered it in fat turn once during cooking so that both top and bottom are crisp.
  If covered in foil remove this for last 30 minutes.
3 Veal MUST be well cooked, otherwise it is very indigestible. If covering the meat with foil, or using a covered roaster, allow an extra 15 minutes' cooking time. Roast in a moderate oven (375°F. – Gas Mark 4).
4 If stuffing veal, weigh after stuffing, so that you include weight of stuffing.
  Since veal is a young meat, the quick method of roasting should be perfectly satisfactory. If you have bought veal that looks older than you might wish, i.e. it is darker in colour, then the slow method of roasting can be used. As you will see from the table, veal is a meat that takes

a long time to cook, and therefore you should allow a little longer by the slow method than for roasting beef or lamb.

Accompaniments to veal

Stuffing will, of course, be cooked in the veal. About half an hour before the veal is cooked either put sausages in the same roasting tin as the veal, pricking them first, or heat a very little fat in another tin and put the sausages in this.

Veal stuffing

no cooking

you will need:

2 oz. shredded suet OR melted margarine	4 oz. breadcrumbs
½ teaspoon mixed herbs	1 egg seasoning
grated rind and juice ¼ lemon	2–3 teaspoons chopped parsley

1 Mix all the ingredients together thoroughly.
2 Cooked meat from giblets can be added if wished. This makes a richer stuffing.

Bacon rolls

You can choose streaky bacon and cut each long rasher in half and remove the rinds. Roll and put on metal skewers, place in the oven about 15 minutes before the veal is cooked.

Rice-stuffed roast cutlets

cooking time: 35–45 minutes

you will need for 4 servings:

2 oz. cooked rice	1 or 2 rashers chopped bacon
1 tablespoon chopped parsley	1 egg
2 tablespoons chopped onion	seasoning
	4 veal cutlets
2 oz. suet	extra butter for foil

1 Mix rice, parsley, onion, suet and bacon together.
2 Add egg, seasoning.
3 Spread on top of each cutlet.
4 Wrap sheets of well-buttered foil round cutlets.
5 Roast for approximately 35–45 minutes in moderately hot oven (400°F. – Gas Mark 5).
6 Serve with extra cooked rice.

Roast fillet of veal

cooking time: according to weight

you will need for 4 servings:

1½–2 lb. loin or breast of veal	butter chipolatas or cocktail sausages
salt and pepper	
little flour	mixed vegetables
4–5 bacon rashers	

1 Ask your butcher to bone and roll the joint of veal.
2 Rub it with seasoned flour and cover with bacon rashers.
3 Wrap in buttered foil and bake in a moderate oven (375°F. – Gas Mark 4) allowing 30 minutes per lb. and 30 minutes over.
4 Half an hour before the meat is cooked fold back the foil and surround the meat with the sausages.
5 Baste sausages and veal from time to time.
6 Serve with a garnish of vegetables.

Veal à la dame blanche

cooking time: according to weight

you will need:
1 joint of fillet or loin of veal

for the sauce:

2 tablespoons vinegar	few peppercorns
2 cloves	¾ pint white sauce (see page 86)
blade of mace	¼ pint aspic jelly
bay leaf	6 tablespoons whipped thick cream
1 tablespoon chopped ham	

1 Roast the veal, see table on page 9, and allow to become completely cold.
2 Meanwhile prepare the sauce.
3 Cook together the vinegar, cloves, mace, bay leaf, ham and peppercorns for 10 minutes. Remove spices and bay leaf.
4 Add the white sauce and reduce until thick.
5 Add the aspic jelly and stir well.
6 Remove from the heat.
7 When cool add the whipped cream.
8 Coat the meat with this, and keep in the refrigerator or a cool place until the sauce is firm.

To roast pork

For the cooking times see the table on page 10. Choose loin, leg, shoulder, blade bone, spare rib.

1 Always rub the fat of pork with melted lard, oil or butter and season before roasting to give a good crackling.
2 See that the loin is evenly and deeply cut (scored); this encourages it to crisp and makes the crackling.
3 Start in a really hot oven (425–450°F. – Gas Mark 6–7), then reduce the heat after the first 30 minutes to moderately hot (400°F. – Gas Mark 5), and cook more slowly.
4 It is possible to roast pork in a very moderate oven, in which case allow 40 minutes per lb. Pork, because of the high fat content, is rarely roasted by the slow method.

Accompaniments to pork

Sage and onion stuffing can either be baked separately or put into the pork, see page 17 for ways of stuffing meat.
Apple sauce is cooked separately (see page 86).

Sage and onion stuffing

cooking time: 20 minutes

you will need:

2 large onions, peeled	1 teaspoon dried sage
½ pint water	1 egg*
4 oz. breadcrumbs	good pinch salt and
1 oz. suet	pepper

*Some of the onion stock may be used instead, this makes a less firm stuffing, which many people prefer.

1 Cook onion with water and seasoning.
2 Simmer steadily for 20 minutes to partially cook onions.
3 Remove from water, cut finely on a chopping board.
4 Transfer to basin and add all other ingredients.

Variations

Sage and ham – omit breadcrumbs, add 4 oz. finely diced ham and crushed clove of garlic.
Onion and tomato – omit sage and add pulp from 3–4 skinned, chopped tomatoes.
Sage and walnut – use no onions but add 4 oz. extra breadcrumbs, grated rind and juice of 1 lemon, 2 oz. chopped walnuts.
Sage and apple – use 1 onion only and 1 large peeled diced apple.

Roast blade bone of pork

cooking time: approximately 2¼ hours

you will need for 6 servings:

4 lb. blade bone of pork	salt and pepper
2 sliced cooking apples	garlic salt
	little lard

1 Ask the butcher to score the skin and remove the bone from the joint, leaving a pocket through the centre.
2 Fill this with the sliced raw apples, seasoned with salt and pepper.
3 Rub the fat with lard.
4 Roast as table on page 10.

Crispy spare ribs with sweet and sour sauce

This is an ideal party dish which is unusual and not too expensive.

cooking time: 50 minutes

you will need for 4 servings:
4–8 spare ribs*

for the sauce:

½ oz. cornflour	1 tablespoon soy
¼ pint and 4 tablespoons water	sauce or Worcestershire sauce
2 tablespoons mixed vinegar pickles	2 good teaspoons brown sugar or golden syrup
2 tablespoons vinegar	
salt and pepper	

to garnish:

cooked rice	wedges lemon

*By using 8 thin chops the fat will be very crisp.

1 Put meat into roasting tin and roast in hot oven (425–450°F. – Gas Mark 6–7) for approximately 30 minutes.
2 Pour off surplus fat and return to oven for further 15–20 minutes until chops are really crisp and brown.
3 Blend cornflour with water, chop pickles fairly

finely, then put all ingredients for sauce into pan and cook until thickened.

4 Make a wide border of rice on a warm dish, arrange the chops on this. Pour the sauce into the centre. Put wedges of lemon round the edge.

Pork chops and gooseberry sauce

cooking time: 20–30 minutes

you will need for 4 servings:

4 spare rib or neck of pork chops	**for the sauce:** 8 oz. gooseberries
salt and pepper	knob of butter
sprig mint	2 oz. sugar
bay leaf	

1 Put the chops in a fireproof dish, season, add mint and bay leaf.
2 Roast in a moderately hot oven (400°F. – Gas Mark 5) for 20–30 minutes.
3 Meanwhile top and tail gooseberries and cook until pulp with butter and sugar. Arrange round chops.

Variations

Farmer's pork chops – serve chops on a bed of cooked cabbage tossed with fried, sliced onions and apple.

With orange – when chops are nearly cooked, add finely grated rind 1 orange, juice 2 oranges and 2–3 tablespoons water.

Roast pork oriental

cooking time: approximately 3 hours

you will need for 8 servings:

4 lb. boned and scored shoulder of pork	1 tablespoon slivered almonds
salt and pepper	1 tablespoon chopped onion
little dry mustard	
4 slices bread	1 tablespoon dried sage
4 tablespoons chopped celery	2 oz. melted butter
	8 small red apples

1 Sprinkle the meat outside and in pocket with salt and pepper and rub with dry mustard.
2 Cut bread into small cubes, or reduce to crumbs.
3 Mix with celery, almonds, onion and sage and toss in the butter.
4 Lightly pack the stuffing into the meat and skewer or tie into shape. (This is a cushion roast, not a roll).

5 Roast in very moderate oven (350°F. – Gas Mark 3) allowing 40 minutes per lb.
6 Baste two or three times with dripping from pan.
7 Serve with baked red apples and oriental mustard, made by beating a little lemon juice into made mustard.

Apricot-stuffed loin of pork

cooking time: according to weight

you will need for 8 servings:

4 lb. loin of pork	2 oz. breadcrumbs
1 large can apricots	seasoning
4 oz. sausage meat	little lard or oil

1 Chine the loin, cut a pocket through fat from side to side.
2 Drain and mash the apricots – leaving 8–10 to garnish.
3 Mix with sausage meat and crumbs, season and press into pocket of meat.
4 Brush scored skin with melted lard or oil, season lightly.
5 Roast as table on page 10.
6 Garnish with apricot halves, serve hot or cold.

Variations

Prune-stuffed loin – Use about 8 oz. cooked prunes instead of apricots.

Festive loin – have two loins of pork – 5 or 6 chops each at least. Chine and score skin. Trim meat away from bone ends, and lock the two loins by bones. Roast according to table. Make stuffing (sage and onion – or one of the variations) into balls, roast for last 20 minutes and serve round meat.

Pineapple-stuffed loin – use 1 large can pineapple rings well drained, instead of apricots.

Pork with raisins and curry sauce

cooking time: 2 hours

you will need for 4 servings:

2 lb. loin of pork	curry sauce, see page 73
salt and pepper	
clove garlic, optional	2 oz. raisins
	cooked rice

1 Season the joint of pork with plenty of salt and pepper.

2 If garlic is liked, cut a clove into slivers and insert in the fat side of the joint.

3 Wrap the meat in foil and roast in a moderate oven (375°F. – Gas Mark 4) for 2 hours.

4 Meanwhile prepare a curry sauce.

5 Pour boiling water over the raisins and allow to stand for 5 minutes. Drain.

6 Serve the pork with rice and drained raisins.

7 The sauce should be served separately.

To roast bacon or ham

The shape of bacon or ham varies a great deal, and this plays a big part in determining the exact cooking time, see the table on page 10. Choose gammon, slipper, middle gammon, back and ribs, joint top streaky.

1 Soak the joint overnight in cold water, for roasting 'keeps in' the salt flavour.

2 While you can roast bacon for the whole of the cooking, it is much more moist and delicious if boiled (or simmered) for half the time. A joint that takes 3 hours to cook would be better simmered for 1½ hours and roasted for the rest of the time.

3 The time needed for cooking bacon depends a great deal on your choice of meat. For roasting choose the better cuts, as above, and for a really prime gammon 20–25 minutes per lb. and 20–25 minutes over is sufficient. As mentioned above, bacon joints vary a great deal in shape. A flat joint will cook through more rapidly than a thick one of the same weight. The heat of the oven also determines the cooking time. The time given assumes a hot oven (425–450°F. – Gas Mark 6–7). If you wish to roast in a moderately hot oven (400°F. – Gas Mark 5), you must allow a minimum of 30 minutes per lb. cooking time and 30 minutes over. A slower oven requires a longer period.

4 If roasting for the entire time, the outside of the bacon could become a little hard so EITHER baste very well, put the joint into a covered roaster or wrap in foil. If you wish the fat to have an appetising brownness unwrap the foil for the last 30 minutes. You can use a hot (425–450°F. – Gas Mark 6–7) or very moderate oven (300–350°F. – Gas Mark 2–3) for this method of roasting.

5 Roast bacon can be glazed afterwards and suggestions for the attractive glazing of ham and bacon are given on page 36. If you wish to have an unglazed roast joint of bacon, here is the best way to encourage the fat to crisp. Remove the skin, score the fat neatly, see page 12, and then brush the fat with a little melted lard or oil.

Accompaniments to bacon or ham

Serve roast bacon with new or roast potatoes – these are better roasted in a separate tin if you have simmered bacon first. See page 22. A thickened gravy, using some of the stock, can be served, see page 18.

Apple sauce and sage and onion stuffing, see page 29, blend well, as with pork – or try **baked apple rings:** core dessert apples, but do not peel, and allow 25–30 minutes in roasting tin.

Bacon and pineapple

cooking time: 2½ hours

you will need for 6–8 servings:

3 lb. piece best-end streaky bacon	1 small can pineapple rings

1 Soak the bacon for about 3 hours.

2 Remove the rind with a sharp knife and make deep incisions across the fat.

3 Insert halves of pineapple rings and pour over a little of the juice.

4 Wrap in aluminium foil and place on a tin.

5 Bake in a moderately hot oven (400°F. – Gas Mark 5) for 2½ hours.*

6 For the last 10 minutes uncover the top and baste with the pineapple juice.

7 Return to a hot oven to glaze.

8 Serve with roast potatoes and peas.

*Or simmer for 1½ hours and roast for remainder of time.

Apricot and orange glazed gammon

cooking time: see method

you will need for 8 servings:

1 joint corner or middle gammon (approx. 4–5 lb.)	3 medium oranges 6 oz. dried apricots 3 oz. brown sugar

1 Soak gammon overnight in cold water (mild cured needs only several hours; sweet cured – none).
2 Cover the bacon in a pan with fresh cold water, and bring to boil.
3 Lower heat and allow to simmer steadily, keeping joint well covered. Allow 20 minutes per lb. and 20 minutes over.
4 After about 1 hour 15 minutes, remove from the water and cool off. Then take off the skin and score fat with a sharp knife.
5 While gammon is cooking prepare the glaze. Grate the rind from oranges and squeeze out the juice. Pour juice over the apricots and simmer, covered, for about 30 minutes. Strain off liquid, and blend with orange rind and sugar.
6 Brush glaze over the gammon and then heat in a moderate oven (375°F. Gas Mark 4–5) for remainder of cooking time (i.e. 35–40 minutes). 15 minutes before serving, press apricots against glaze.

Bacon with sage and apple stuffing

cooking time: 2 hours

you will need for 6 servings:

1 joint forehock, about 3 lb. sage and apple stuffing, see page 29	water 1 good tablespoon marmalade about 12–18 cloves

1 Lay bacon flat.
2 Spread with stuffing, roll and skewer or tie firmly.
3 Place joint in pan, cover with water and bring to the boil.
4 Lower heat, simmer gently for 1½ hours.
5 Skin joint, score fat in diamond pattern with sharp knife, brush with the marmalade, stud centre of each diamond with a clove.
6 Roast in a hot oven (425–450°F. – Gas Mark 6–7) for 20–30 minutes.

Roast ham with pineapple

cooking time: according to weight

you will need for 8–14 servings:

1 ham, 3–5 lb. 1 carrot 1 onion 1 piece of celery 1 bay leaf 8 peppercorns	approximately 12–18 cloves 2 tablespoons brown sugar 2 teaspoons mustard 1 large can pineapple slices

1 Soak the ham for 24 hours.
2 Calculate the cooking time at 20–25 minutes per lb. and 20–25 minutes over. For a 5 lb. ham the cooking time is 2–2¼ hours.
3 Place in saucepan of simmering water with vegetables, bay leaf and peppercorns and simmer for 1–1¼ hours.
4 Remove from water and bake in hot oven (420°F. – Gas Mark 6) for 40 minutes.
5 Remove from oven and strip off brown skin. Score the fat in a diamond pattern and place a clove in each diamond.
6 Cover top of ham with a mixture of brown sugar and mustard, pressing in well.
7 Drain the pineapple and baste the ham with the juice. Dredge with more brown sugar.
8 Surround ham with pineapple slices and return to oven for about 20 minutes or until the top is crisply browned.

Hawaiian gammon

cooking time: 30 minutes

you will need for 4 servings:

4 slices gammon 1 inch thick 1 small can pineapple slices 4 cloves corn oil 12 glacé cherries, use fresh if in season	mint leaves parsley **for sauce:** 1 level teaspoon dry mustard 1 level teaspoon cornflour 1 tablespoon water

1 Trim the rind from the gammon.
2 Arrange four slices of pineapple on top.
3 Spike the gammon fat with the cloves. Brush with corn oil.
4 Place in an ovenproof dish. Pour over the pineapple juice from the can.
5 Bake for 20–30 minutes in a moderately hot oven (400°F. – Gas Mark 5).
6 When cooked remove cloves and put gammon and pineapple on serving dish.

7 Decorate with cherries and mint leaves.
8 Garnish with parsley. Keep hot. Serve with sauce.

Pineapple mustard sauce

1 Mix mustard and cornflour to a paste with 1 tablespoon water.
2 Add juices from the oven dish.
3 Cook for 3 minutes on top of cooker. Season if liked.

Fruited bacon

cooking time: according to weight

you will need for 14–16 servings:

5–6 lb. gammon	2 oz. brown sugar
cloves to taste	¼ pint water
4 tablespoons clear honey	3 cooking apples

1 Soak the bacon overnight.
2 Either put into a pan of water and simmer, see page 72, or roast, uncovered, in a very moderate oven (300–350°F. – Gas Mark 2–3) for about 3 hours.
3 When cooked remove rind, score the fat and stud with cloves.
4 Heat honey, sugar and water.
5 Put bacon in roasting tin over peeled, cored, sliced apples, and pour over honey mixture.
6 Roast for final 20 minutes in moderately hot oven (400°F. – Gas Mark 5).

Variation

Honey roast ham – recipe as above, using ham or bacon.
Spread fat thickly with honey before studding with cloves and roast for 20 minutes.

To Bake Meat

Baking and roasting are similar and one method often becomes a modification of the other. In both the food is cooked in the oven.
Roast meat is most usually cooked with fat, or for pot roasting a little stock or water is added. Meat can be baked in a variety of ways. Some examples are, for instance, in a sauce, as one of the ingredients for stuffing a vegetable like marrow, or in a pie or pasty.

Bobotie

This meat dish from South Africa is an excellent way to turn minced beef or mutton into a rather unusual dish. The almonds can be omitted if wished.

cooking time: 1 hour

you will need for 4 servings:

1 oz. dripping or fat	thick slices of bread, about 4 oz.
2 sliced onions	
1 good tablespoon curry powder	¼ pint milk
	1½ lb. minced beef OR mutton
1 teaspoon salt	
2 teaspoons sugar	1 large or 2 small eggs
1 tablespoon vinegar OR lemon juice	few chopped almonds, optional

1 Heat the fat in a frying pan and cook the onions until soft, then add the curry powder, salt, sugar, vinegar or lemon juice and mix thoroughly.
2 Put the bread into a dish and pour the milk over it. Let it stand for 15 minutes, then pour off and keep any of the milk not absorbed by the bread.
3 Beat the bread until very soft, then add this to the fried onion mixture, together with the meat and one small egg or half a large egg.
4 Grease a dish and pour the mixture in.
5 Pour the milk left from soaking the bread over the rest of the egg, and cover the meat mixture with this custard.
6 Cook in the centre of a moderately hot oven (400°F. – Gas Mark 5) for 30 minutes, then reduce the heat to very moderate (350°F. – Gas Mark 3) for a further 30 minutes.
7 Decorate with the chopped almonds.

Note

You can use cooked meat for this dish, although the flavour is not so good. Cook for 25 minutes only.

Lasagna

cooking time: 1¼ hours

you will need for 4 servings:

4–6 oz. lasagna (the broad flat ribbon pasta)
6 oz. sliced Cheddar cheese

approximately 4 oz. cream cheese
little grated Parmesan cheese

for the sauce:

2 oz. butter
1 onion
2 oz. mushrooms
1 carrot
4 oz. bacon

1 small can tomato purée and ¼ pint and 4 tablespoons water or stock or 8 oz. fresh tomatoes and ½ pint stock
4–6 oz. minced beef
salt and pepper

1 Cook the lasagna in plenty of boiling salted water until soft.
2 To make the sauce, heat butter in pan.
3 Fry the chopped onion, chopped mushrooms and finely chopped carrot.
4 Add the diced bacon and fry for a further few minutes.
5 Put in the tomato purée, stock or water and meat, bring to the boil. Season. Cook steadily until mixture thickens and the meat is cooked.
6 When the lasagna is cooked, strain carefully from the water and allow to dry for a while, then cut into neat lengths.
7 Put a layer of lasagna, a layer of meat sauce, then a layer of thinly sliced Cheddar cheese, cream cheese and a sprinkling of Parmesan cheese.
8 Add another layer of lasagna, the rest of the meat sauce, more lasagna, and a final layer of the cheese, ending with sliced Cheddar cheese.
9 Put into a moderately hot oven (400°F. – Gas Mark 5) for approximately 30 minutes until golden brown.
10 Serve with green vegetables or a crisp salad.

Variations

With sherry – instead of using the bacon and meat sauce use all meat in a similar mixture. You can vary this by making it more highly flavoured, using a little sherry, adding chopped green pepper, a little crushed garlic.

With different cheeses – you can vary the flavour of the cheeses. It is more correct to use Gruyère cheese instead of Cheddar.

With Mozzarella – instead of a British cream cheese use Mozzarella, if it is available.

With sauce bolognese – use sauce bolognese, see page 85.

Stuffed marrow

cooking time: 1½–1¾ hours

you will need for 4 servings:

1 medium-sized marrow
4 oz. long-grain rice
1 tablespoon oil
1 small onion, finely chopped
2 oz. mushrooms, finely chopped
8 oz. raw minced beef

2 level tablespoons chopped parsley
seasoning
1 egg

to garnish:
few cooked peas and pimento, optional

1 Cut the top off the marrow lengthwise, scoop out the seeds.
2 Cook the rice in boiling salted water until tender, drain well.
2 Heat the oil, sauté the onion for a few minutes.
4 Add the mushrooms and beef and cook a further 5 minutes.
5 Remove from the heat and add the parsley and rice.
6 Mix well and season to taste.
7 Bind with the beaten egg.
8 Fill the centre of the marrow with the stuffing mixture.
9 Replace the top and wrap completely in foil.
10 Place in a baking tin and cook for approximately 1–1¼ hours in a moderate oven (375°F. – Gas Mark 4).
11 Garnish with peas and strips of pimento, if liked.

Variations

The meat mixture can be varied:
1 by using **tomatoes** in place of mushrooms.
2 by adding a little **crushed garlic** or garlic salt for a more definite flavour.

Other vegetables can be stuffed with a meat mixture. Bake at the same temperature as marrow.

Stuffed aubergines – simmer the aubergines or egg plant in boiling salted water for about

10 minutes. Split through the centre. Remove the pulp, blend with the stuffing and bake for 25–30 minutes in a greased tin in the oven.

Stuffed courgettes – the tiny marrows can be stuffed in exactly the same way, but you have no need to pre-cook, and the centre of the halved courgettes can be added to the meat mixture.

Stuffed onions – peel and cook really large onions for about 15 minutes in salted water. Lift out and carefully remove the centre. Chop. Add to the stuffing. Pile into the centre of the onions. Wrap in greased foil or cook in a greased covered dish for approximately 1–1¼ hours.

Stuffed red or green peppers – boil for approximately 5–10 minutes in salted water. Halve, remove centre seeds and core. Fill with stuffing and bake for approximately 30 minutes.

7 To prepare the sauce, melt the butter, stir in the flour and cook gently for 1–2 minutes.
8 Add milk and bring to the boil, stirring all the time. Season.
9 Pour over the top of the prepared dish and top with the remaining cheese.
10 Bake in centre of a moderate oven (375°F. – Gas Mark 4) for approximately 30 minutes until golden brown.

Variation

Economical moussaka – omit the aubergines and use about 1½ lb. thinly sliced potatoes instead.

Moussaka

cooking time: 1 hour 5 minutes

you will need for 4 servings:

1 tablespoon oil	4 aubergines
1 lb. minced lean mutton or beef	4 tablespoons oil for frying
1 large onion, chopped	(approximately)
salt and cayenne pepper	6 oz. grated cheese
2 level tablespoons tomato purée	**for the sauce:**
1 beef stock cube dissolved in 3 tablespoons hot water or use brown stock	1 oz. butter
	1 oz. flour
	½ pint milk
	salt and pepper

1 Heat 1 tablespoon oil, add meat and onion and brown.
2 Season with salt and cayenne pepper. Stir in the tomato purée and the stock, and simmer for 30 minutes.
3 Peel and thinly slice the aubergines and fry lightly in 4 tablespoons oil.
4 Put a layer in the base of an ovenproof dish and sprinkle thickly with some of the cheese.
5 Cover with a second layer of aubergines and cheese, then with the meat mixture.
6 Top with further layers of aubergines and cheese, keeping back approximately 1 oz. cheese for the top.

Swiss steak

cooking time: 1½ hours

you will need for 4 servings:

2 oz. butter	black pepper
1 clove garlic, optional	3 tablespoons wine
1 packet soup powder*	4 oz. mushrooms
1 lb. rump steak 1 inch thick	

*Use a soup powder with a pronounced flavour – mushroom, tomato, pea and ham; this acts as thickening and seasoning.

1 Spread 1 oz. of the butter over the centre of a piece of foil and rub with cut clove garlic, if wished.
2 Shake the packet of soup well and sprinkle half over the butter.
3 Place the piece of steak on this.
4 Sprinkle a little black pepper on the steak, then the remainder of the soup mix.
5 Pour the wine over this.
6 Slice the mushrooms and arrange round the steak with the crushed garlic.
7 Fold the foil and make into a parcel to prevent juices running out.
8 Bake for approximately 1½ hours in a moderate oven (375°F. – Gas Mark 4).

35

Crumbed veal Nanetta

cooking time: 30 minutes

you will need for 4 servings:

4 escalopes veal
little prepared mustard
4 thin slices ham,
  same size as veal
1 egg
1 tablespoon milk
4 tablespoons soft
  breadcrumbs

1 tablespoon grated
  Parmesan or sharp
  dry Cheddar cheese
little oil or butter for
  frying
2 tablespoons wine or
  tomato juice

1 Pound escalopes until thin and spread lightly with prepared mustard.
2 Place slices of ham on each.
3 Dip in beaten egg and milk and then in mixture of breadcrumbs and cheese.
4 Pat coating on firmly.
5 Fry gently in oil or butter until brown on both sides.
6 Place in buttered ovenproof dish.
7 Sprinkle lightly with wine or tomato juice.
8 Cook in moderate oven (375°F. – Gas Mark 4) for 20 minutes.

To bake bacon or ham in a pastry crust

The old-fashioned way of cooking bacon or ham, which keeps it very moist, is in a pastry crust.

you will need:

bacon or ham
flour

water

1 Prepare the bacon or ham as for roasting, i.e. soaking overnight.
2 If wished, you can cook for half the time by boiling, although it is not necessary by this particular method, which does keep the bacon or ham very moist.
3 Make a flour and water paste. To cover a joint of approximately 6 lb. in weight, you will need approximately 1 lb. flour and a good ¼ pint water at least.
4 Roll out the flour and water dough to make a really neat parcel.
5 Wrap the bacon or ham in this, allow 20–25 minutes per lb. for prime cuts of bacon or ham, with an extra 45 minutes to 1 hour for the heat to penetrate through the flour paste.

6 Start in a hot oven (425–450°F. – Gas Mark 6–7), and reduce the heat to moderately hot (400°F. – Gas Mark 5) after the first hour.
7 If you are doubtful as to the quality of the ham or bacon, it is advisable to allow 45 minutes per lb., plus 45 minutes to 1 hour at a moderate heat (375°F. – Gas Mark 4).
8 To serve, strip away the casing, and glaze the bacon, if wished.

Variation

Bacon in a jacket – instead of flour and water crust, use about 2 oz. fine oatmeal to each 8–10 oz. flour, rub in a little fat, bind with egg and water. This crust is delicious to eat.

Glazes for bacon and ham

Bacon and ham can be given an infinite variety of glazes to give colour and added flavour.
Most fruits blend well with the glaze for bacon.

Other glazes

1 Mix a little **spice** with **brown sugar**, press into the fat.
2 Brush the fat with **honey,** and sprinkle with a little cinnamon if wished.
3 Blend **brown sugar** with enough **pineapple syrup** to give a paste consistency. Spread over the fat.
4 Stud the fat with **cloves** and sprinkle with a little **white or brown sugar** and breadcrumbs.
Having put on the glaze, bake for about 20 minutes or until a good colour in a moderately hot oven (400°F. – Gas Mark 5).

The following recipe for cherry bacon can be varied by using pineapple, peaches and other fruits.

Cherry bacon

Stud the fat of a cooked piece of bacon with canned, stoned cherries and sprinkle with sugar. Bake as above.

Stuffed gammon steaks

cooking time: 40–50 minutes

you will need for 4 servings:

2 slices gammon, ½ inch thick, each enough for 2 persons	**for the sauce:** 1 tablespoon oil ½ oz. cornflour ½ pint cider 4 cloves seasoning
for the stuffing: 1 small cooking apple, chopped 1 oz. soft breadcrumbs 1 oz. raisins 1 oz. hazelnuts	½ teaspoon made mustard 2 tablespoons honey 1 dessertspoon oil

1 Mix the apple, breadcrumbs, raisins, hazelnuts and mustard together.
2 Heat the honey and oil together.
3 Use to moisten the dry ingredients.
4 Soak the gammon in cold water to remove some of the salt.
5 Cut the rind off. Snip the edges at 2-inch intervals to prevent curling.
6 Place one piece of gammon in a greased baking dish.
7 Spread the stuffing over and place the second slice on top.
8 Heat the oil. Add the cornflour and cook for 1 minute.
9 Add the cider and cloves and bring to the boil, stirring constantly.
10 Add a little seasoning, remembering that the gammon will be slightly salty.
11 Remove the cloves and pour the sauce over the gammon.
12 Bake in a moderately hot oven (400°F. – Gas Mark 5) for about 40–50 minutes, or until the gammon is tender.

Sausage and bacon surprise

cooking time: approximately 20 minutes

you will need for 4 servings:

1 lb. pork sausage meat 4 small eggs 1 teaspoon mixed herbs or basil	salt and pepper 4 rashers streaky bacon

1 Divide the sausage meat into four and place on baking tin.

2 Press a wet cup into each and press the sides up to form hollow.
3 Remove the cup and break an egg into each.
4 Sprinkle with herbs, season with salt and pepper, then cover with halved rashers of bacon.
5 Bake in a moderately hot oven (400°F. – Gas Mark 5) for 15–20 minutes.
6 Serve with crispy potatoes.

Toad-in-the-hole

cooking time: 35–40 minutes

you will need for 4 servings:

½ pint pancake batter (see page 52) 1 oz. fat or clarified dripping	approximately 1 lb. halved kidneys or chops or slices of bacon or liver

1 Make the batter and allow to stand if wished.
2 Put the fat into the tin and heat for about 4 minutes, add the pieces of meat and heat for 8–10 minutes according to size.
3 Pour over the batter and cook in a very hot oven (450°F. – Gas Mark 7–8) until beginning to rise. Lower heat to moderate (375°F. – Gas Mark 4–5) and bake until golden brown.

To cook meat in paper or en papillote

This is a chef's method of cooking which retains a great deal of the flavour of meat.

Insert the prepared tender cutlets, chops or pieces of meat into well-buttered paper bags, seal and put into a hot oven (425–450°F. – Gas Mark 6–7) for approximately 20–30 minutes. The timing, of course, depends on the thickness of the meat.

Meat Pies

A meat pie is a favourite throughout the year. Many are ideal served cold for picnic meals in summer. Normally a pie is covered with some form of pastry, but in this chapter you will find some have a covering of potatoes, which makes a pleasant change.

It must be remembered, when covering a pie with pastry, that you have to be sure that the filling is adequately cooked by the time the pastry is crisp and brown. This can be achieved by pre-cooking the meat, and making absolutely certain that it is cool, and not steaming, before covering with pastry. If you cover steaming hot meat with pastry, it becomes soggy.

If it is more convenient to put uncooked meat into the pie, you must set the pastry in a hot oven, then lower the heat so that the pie cooks through very slowly and gently.

Amounts of pastry

Where a recipe states 8 oz. short crust or 8 oz. suet crust pastry, it means that the pastry is made with 8 oz. flour and the other ingredients in proportion.

Pastry with meat

Meat and pastry together make an excellent combination, the dish is substantial and good-flavoured tender meat with crisp pastry is delicious. A good plan is to use meat fats, in particular lard, as part or all of the fat in the pastry.

Variations

1 If you like a very crisp firm pastry for meat pies, use a mixture of margarine and cooking fat.
2 If you like a very tender melt-in-the-mouth pastry, use all cooking fat or lard.
3 If you wish to make pies or pasties for a picnic use slightly less than the full amount of fat. The pastry will not be so rich but it will be easier to carry.

Beef pie

cooking time: 2½ hours

you will need for 4 servings:

1 lb. stewing steak, cubed	seasoning
1 sliced onion	5 potatoes
4 oz. sliced mushrooms	4 oz. plain flour
3 sliced carrots	¼ teaspoon baking powder
¾ pint stock	2 oz. suet
	little water

1 Put the meat, onion, mushrooms and carrots into a casserole.
2 Pour the stock over and season well.
3 Cook for 1½ hours in a very moderate oven (350°F. – Gas Mark 3), then add the peeled and sliced potatoes.
4 Cook for 20 minutes.
5 Make the pastry top by mixing the flour, baking powder and suet with water.
6 Roll out to cover top of casserole and bake for another 40 minutes.

Cornish pasties

cooking time: 45–50 minutes

you will need:

8 oz. short crust pastry	1 onion
8 oz. beef steak*	salt
4 oz. kidney or liver	pepper
2 raw potatoes	

*Preferably rump steak

1 Roll out the pastry and cut into large rounds with a saucer or tea plate.
2 Chop the meat and liver or kidney finely.
3 Peel the potatoes and onion and slice thinly.
4 Mix the meat and vegetables together, adding salt and pepper.
5 Place the mixture in the centre of the pastry rounds, sprinkling with a little water. Brush the pastry edges with water.
6 Bring the edges up together over the filling. Press gently together. Flute in the traditional Cornish pasty way.
7 Make sure you seal the pastry completely so that the steam cannot escape and the contents cook in their own juice.

8 Cook in a hot oven (425–450°F. – Gas Mark 6–7) for 15 minutes, then lower the temperature a little and cook for a further 30–35 minutes.

Variations

Use corned beef – grate the potato and onion as the meat only needs heating. Mix together with seasoning, mixed herbs if wished, and 2–3 tablespoons gravy or stock. The cooking time need only be approximately 40 minutes.

Omit kidney or liver – kidney or liver in a Cornish pasty is not an essential. Many people would prefer to omit this.

With swede or parsnip – a little diced swede or parsnip can be added to the potato and onion, which should also be diced.

Lamb and celery pasty

cooking time: 45 minutes

you will need for 4 servings:

8 oz. short crust pastry	medium can celery soup
12 oz. cooked lamb	little milk to glaze

1 Make the pastry. Halve, and roll each half into a 7–7½-inch round.
2 Place one round of pastry on a tin or ovenproof dish, cover with the diced or minced lamb and half the soup. Put the second circle of pastry on top, seal and neaten the edges and decorate with pastry leaves. Brush with the milk.
3 Bake in a moderately hot oven (400°F. – Gas Mark 5–6) and serve with rest of the soup as a sauce.

Potato cheese pie

cooking time: 1¼–1½ hours

you will need for 4 servings:

1 lb. potatoes	1 lb. raw minced beef
1 large chopped onion	
1–2 tablespoons chopped parsley	2 medium-sized grated carrots
salt and pepper	a little grated cheese

1 Grate the potatoes.
2 Mix all the ingredients together in a bowl except the cheese.
3 Season to taste and turn into a shallow pie dish.

4 Sprinkle with cheese and bake in a moderately hot oven (400°F. – Gas Mark 5) for about 1¼–1½ hours.

Variation

With leeks – add 2–3 chopped leeks instead of onion and use 1 carrot only.

Sailor pie

cooking time: 3 hours 40 minutes

you will need for 4 servings:

1 lb. chuck steak	seasoning
1 onion	sprig thyme
1 turnip	¼ pint brown ale
1 carrot	¼ pint water
1 tablespoon flour	4 oz. suet pastry

1 Put the chopped meat and vegetables in layers in a casserole with flour and seasoning.
2 Add the thyme, ale and water, cover, and cook for 3 hours in a very moderate oven (325°F. – Gas Mark 2).
3 Place pastry over top, cover again, put oven up to 350°F. – Gas Mark 3 for another ½ hour.
4 Cook for a further 10 minutes.

Steak and kidney pie

cooking time: 1 hour 55 minutes

you will need for 4 servings:

1–1½ lb. stewing steak	½ teaspoon salt
2 lamb's or sheep's kidneys or about 4 oz. ox kidney	1 level teaspoon flour
	water or stock
good pinch pepper	6 oz. rough puff or short crust pastry

1 Cut the steak and kidney into small pieces and roll in the seasoned flour, or, for a very professional effect, cut thin narrow strips of the stewing steak, cut the kidney in tiny pieces. Put a piece of kidney on each strip of stewing steak and roll firmly, then toss in seasoned flour.
2 Stand a pie support or egg cup in the centre of the dish to support the pastry.
3 Put the meat into the pie dish and if not rolling the kidney in the steak, make sure the kidney is well distributed.
4 Pour over enough water or stock to come halfway up the meat. Do not put more, otherwise it may boil out in cooking.
5 Roll out the pastry and cover the pie.

6 If you have any scraps of pastry left form these into leaves and a rose to decorate the pie; it is traditional to ornament savoury pies in this way.

7 Brush the top of the pie over with a very little milk, sticking the rose and leaves in position.

8 Make a tiny slit on the pastry over the pie support or egg cup to allow the steam to escape.

9 Bake in the centre of a hot oven (450°F. – Gas Mark 7) for about 25 minutes to give the pastry a chance to rise.

10 Put a piece of paper over the top of the pie and lower the heat to very moderate (350°F. – Gas Mark 3) to make sure the meat is cooked. Allow about a further 1½ hours.

11 When serving, have a sauce boat of hot stock available to pour into the pie to make extra gravy, if you wish.

Another method of cooking a steak and kidney pie, and many people prefer this because the pastry does not become over-cooked, is as follows:

1 Cut the meat into small pieces and season and flour.

2 Toss in a little fat until lightly brown.

3 Simmer in a little water until nearly tender.

4 Put in the pie dish, allow to cool slightly.

5 Cover with the pastry and bake for 30–40 minutes.

Variations

Steak and mushroom – use sliced mushrooms instead of kidney.

Steak and onion – use small whole or sliced, large onions instead of kidney.

Steak, kidney and oyster – add about eight small oysters to meat, etc.

Using other meats

Redcurrant lamb pie – use middle neck of lamb chop instead of steak, fill dish with layers of seasoned meat and redcurrants. Cover with pastry and bake as steak and kidney pie, allowing about 1 hour 55 minutes cooking time.

Veal pie – use diced fillet of veal, with diced lean bacon, flavoured by one or two gherkins and sliced onion.

Veal cream pie – simmer diced veal with chopped onion in water until tender. Put into thick white sauce with few sliced mushrooms, seasoning, little sherry. Cover with pastry and cook as steak and kidney pie.

Pork and apple pie – use diced fillet of pork instead of steak, and diced cooking apples, tossed in a little sugar and chopped sage instead of kidney.

Pork and prune pie – use diced fillet pork and chopped prunes with a pinch of ginger.

Veal and ham pie

cooking time: 2–2¼ hours

you will need for 4 servings:

12 oz. hot water crust pastry	7 tablespoons water or bone stock
1¼ lb. fillet of veal	beaten egg for glazing
6 oz. ham	1 level teaspoon gelatine
salt and pepper	
½ level teaspoon grated lemon rind	½ level teaspoon meat extract
1–2 hard-boiled eggs	

1 Make pastry and keep warm in a basin until ready to use.

2 Remove pastry from basin and with two-thirds of the dough line a 6-inch cake tin or 1 lb. loaf tin.

3 Wash and dry the meats, removing any skin, and cut into 1-inch cubes.

4 Roll the meats together in salt and pepper and lemon rind.

5 Line the tin with pastry and place half the meat in the bottom. Cut the eggs into halves, place on top of the meat, cover with remaining meat.

6 Pour three tablespoons of the water or stock into the pie.

7 Turn the top edge of pastry-lining in over the meat, damp it all round, roll out remaining third of pastry to make a lid.

8 Press down well all round the edge and cut at ½-inch intervals with a sharp knife to secure.

9 Make a hole in the centre, brush over with beaten egg, decorate with pastry leaves and brush with beaten egg again.

10 Place in centre of a moderate oven (375°F. – Gas Mark 4) for 2–2¼ hours.

11 Leave to cool.

12 Melt the gelatine in remaining water or stock and stir in the meat extract.

13 When the pie is cool and the gelatine mixture just setting, pour into the pie through the hole in the centre and leave to set before serving.

Variation

With peas – instead of hard-boiled eggs use cooked peas to make a layer between meat.

Golden pork roll

cooking time: 1 hour 35 minutes

you will need for 4 servings:

12 oz. short crust pastry	1 piece swede
1–1½ lb. belly of pork	1–2 raw potatoes
1 onion	1 small apple, optional
2 tomatoes	little seasoning
few mushrooms	pinch sage
1–2 raw carrots	very little stock
	beaten egg to glaze

1 Make pastry, roll out to oblong 10 × 8 inches.

2 Cut meat, vegetables and peeled and cored apple into small pieces.

3 Put into a basin and mix well, adding seasoning, sage and a few DROPS stock or water to moisten.

4 Put on to pastry, keeping away from edges.

5 Turn in top and bottom ends, i.e. shorter sides to keep in filling.

6 Form into a neat roll, sealing the edges firmly.

7 Lift on to baking tin and glaze thoroughly with beaten egg.

8 Bake for approximately 20 minutes in centre of a hot oven (425–450°F. – Gas Mark 6–7) to set pastry, then lower heat to moderate (375°F. – Gas Mark 4) and leave for further 1¼ hours to cook filling.

9 If necessary protect pastry with little greaseproof paper during the last stages of cooking.

10 If wished this can be formed into large pasty.

Raised pork pie

cooking time: 2–2¼ hours

you will need for 4–6 servings:

12 oz. hot water crust pastry	**for the jelly:** pork bones or pork trotter
for the filling:	2 pints water
1¼ lb. shoulder pork	1 onion
1 teaspoon powdered sage	seasoning
salt and pepper	1 teaspoon gelatine
beaten egg	

1 Make the pastry, and use two-thirds to line tin, see Veal and ham pie, page 40.

2 Put on to greased baking sheet, and fill with diced pork, sage and seasoning.

3 Roll out remaining third of pastry, brush the edges of the pie with beaten egg, press the lid on firmly to seal.

4 Use trimmings to form leaves for decoration, brush with beaten egg, making a hole in the centre of the lid. Bake as Veal and ham pie.

5 Make a jelly from the bones, water, onion and seasoning by boiling for about 2 hours.

6 Strain, add the dissolved gelatine and cool.

7 Pour some of this into hole in the lid, when pie is cool, and leave to set before cutting.

Meat cobbler

cooking time: 20–25 minutes

you will need for 4 servings:

large can stewed steak	1½ oz. butter or margarine
6 oz. self raising flour	milk to mix
seasoning	

1 Put the meat into an ovenproof dish and heat for 5 minutes.

2 Sieve flour and seasoning, rub in butter or margarine and bind to a soft rolling consistency with milk.

3 Roll out and cut into neat rounds. Arrange on top of meat and bake for 15–20 minutes in a hot oven (425–450°F. – Gas Mark 6–7).

Meat Puddings

A really good meat pudding is an ideal dish for a hungry family. It has the great advantage that it can be left unattended, except for filling up the water in the pan or in the steamer.

Here are points to remember:
1 Fill the basin full of meat, but not to come above the top of the basin. If you do some of the juice is likely to boil out during cooking.

2 Allow ample time for cooking a meat pudding. It is not a dish that can be hurried.

3 If you wish the pudding to cook in the minimum time, use cooked or partially cooked meat. The best-flavoured pudding is made with un-cooked meat, for all meat juices are sealed in.

4 Make certain that the water boils really rapidly for at least the first hour to 1½ hours of the cooking time. In this way you ensure a light crust. At the end of this time you can lower the heat.

5 Always cover the top of a meat pudding care-fully with either well-greased greaseproof paper or well-greased foil.

6 Take care when you lift a pudding out of the steamer or pan that you do not scald yourself. Make string loops.

To line a pudding basin with suet crust pastry

1 Make the suet pastry.

2 Roll out the dough to ¼ inch thick on a lightly floured board.

3 Form into a circle and cut out a quarter and put on one side for the lid.

4 Lift the other piece into a lightly greased basin and arrange. You will find that it should fit very well. The pudding basin is neatly lined without surplus folds of pastry giving an uneven surface.

5 If you prefer another method, insert the com-plete circle of pastry into the basin, and gently pull the pastry so that it forms an even layer.

6 Cut off the surplus top edge, being very careful to allow enough pastry for the pastry lid to be sealed to this. Use the surplus pastry for the lid.

To cover the top of a suet pudding

1 Roll the pastry for the lid to a round large enough to cover the top of the basin. Seal the top and side pastry edges by brushing each with a little cold water and pinching them firmly together with your fingers.

2 Grease a piece of greaseproof paper well.

3 Lay the greased side over the pudding, making a pleat across the centre. This enables the pastry

to rise. If the greased, greaseproof paper is not pleated it restricts the pastry rising.

4 Either tuck in the edges very firmly or secure with string.

To tuck greaseproof paper over a suet pudding

1 Hold the paper over the pudding with one hand.

2 With the other hand twist the edge of the paper firmly and tuck under the rim.

3 Continue in this way all round the pudding until you have formed a tight ridge.

4 To make sure the paper stays firmly in position, it is a good idea to cover it either with another piece of greaseproof paper or, better still, with foil.

5 In the old days a floured pudding cloth was used, but most people prefer to dispense with pudding cloths, since they have to be boiled, dried and kept clean.

6 This method of covering without string is per-fectly all right if you know you can remove the pudding from the steamer or the saucepan easily. It does mean you must have a good space round the basin so that your hands, protected by a cloth, can get a good grip of the very hot basin.

7 In most cases, therefore, it is better to put a string loop on the basin for easy removal.

String supports for steamed puddings

1 Tie string very firmly round the top of the pudding basin.

2 Test to see that it will not slip as you form the string handle.

3 Having made sure the string is holding the paper or foil firmly in position, insert one end of another long piece of string into this.

4 Tie very firmly.

5 Bring the string over the top of the pudding quite loosely.

6 Insert and tie firmly into the string round the basin, leaving more than enough to bring back again so that there is a double loop of string over the basin to form the basis of the handle.

7 Now twist the remainder of the length of the string over and over these two loops to form a firm, safe handle that will support the weight of the pudding.

Rabbit and mushroom pudding

cooking time: 3 hours

you will need for 4 servings:

10 oz. suet crust pastry	4 bacon rashers
1 rabbit	4 oz. mushrooms
seasoning	2 small onions
1 oz. flour	1 teaspoon sage

1 Make the suet crust pastry.
2 Cut the rabbit into meat joints and coat with well seasoned flour. Chop the bacon, mushrooms and onions.
3 Line a greased basin with some of the pastry, and roll out the remaining pastry to form a lid.
4 Fill the pudding with the rabbit, bacon, mushrooms and onions, sage and enough water to cover the meat. Damp the edges and press the lid on. Cover with greased greaseproof paper and foil.
5 Steam for 3 hours.

Sea pie

cooking time: about 2 hours 30 minutes

you will need for 4 servings:

1 oz. fat	1 pint stock OR water
2 onions	and a stock cube
8 oz.–1 lb. stewing steak	4–6 carrots
	turnip
½ oz. flour	4 oz. suet crust pastry
seasoning	

1 Heat fat in pan and fry chopped onions for a few minutes.
2 Cut meat into neat pieces and coat in seasoned flour, then cook in the fat for a few minutes.
3 Gradually add stock.
4 Bring to the boil, add diced carrots and turnip with extra seasoning if required. Simmer gently for approximately 2 hours.
5 Make the suet crust pastry.
6 Roll into a round the size of the saucepan and place on top of the meat mixture, first making certain there is plenty of liquid in the pan.
7 If saucepan lid is deep enough to allow for

mixture rising without sticking to pastry, put on, otherwise leave uncovered.
8 Cook steadily for approximately 30 minutes.

Variation
With leeks – instead of onions use 8 oz. leeks, and for other vegetables, 1 carrot and 4 parsnips (sliced).

Steak and kidney pudding

cooking time: 3½–4 hours

you will need for 4 servings:

for the pastry:	4 oz. ox kidney
8 oz. suet crust pastry	2 tablespoons seasoned flour
for the filling:	2 tablespoons stock or water
12 oz.–1 lb. stewing steak*	

*For large appetites you can allow up to 1¼ lb. stewing steak.

1 Make pastry and turn on to a lightly floured board.
2 Roll out two-thirds thinly, as this pastry rises.
3 Line a well-greased 1½ pint size pudding basin with this.
4 Put in the steak and kidney (cut into small pieces and rolled in the seasoned flour) and add the cold water or stock.
5 Roll out the remaining pastry to form the lid. Brush the edges with cold water, cover the pudding and press together to seal.
6 Cover with greased paper or foil and steam for 3½–4 hours.
7 For a good result, make sure that the water is boiling rapidly when the pudding goes on, and always replenish with boiling water.
8 The heat may be reduced after first 1½ hours when the crust will have risen.

Because it is completely enclosed, the flavour of the meat in a steak and kidney pudding is particularly delicious. If you do not want the pastry, the following recipe will give the same flavour.

Basin steak and kidney

cooking time: 4–5 hours

you will need for 4 servings:

1 lb. stewing steak (skirt is best)	1 tablespoon seasoned flour
4 oz. ox kidney	

1 Dice meat and kidney and roll in seasoned flour.
2 Put into basin and add enough water to cover meat.
3 Put a piece of greaseproof paper or foil over top of basin and seal tightly.
4 Stand basin in steamer over gently boiling water and cook for 4–5 hours.
5 Chopped onion, herbs or garlic salt can be added for a change.

Variations

Steak and vegetables – mix diced or whole vegetables – celery, onions, carrots, little swede, parsnip or turnip with meat.

Steak and mushroom pudding – omit the kidney and add 1 sliced onion and 4 oz. sliced mushrooms.

Bacon winter roll

cooking time: 1 hour 30 minutes

you will need for 4 servings:

10 oz. flour (with plain flour use 1½ teaspoons baking powder)	milk
	8 oz. minced bacon
	1 minced onion
4 oz. grated lard or shredded suet	1 minced carrot
	ground black pepper
¼ teaspoon salt	

1 Mix the flour, fat and salt together to a stiff dough with milk.

2 Roll out to an oblong and spread with mixture of bacon, onion and carrot.
3 Sprinkle with pepper and make a roll, sealing the edges.
4 Wrap in a floured cloth or a piece of greased foil (make a pleat to allow for swelling) and boil for 1½ hours.
5 Serve with tomato sauce, see page 85.

Savoury apple and bacon pudding

cooking time: 3 hours

you will need for 4 servings:

8 oz. suet crust pastry	4 oz. cabbage heart, optional, or 2 oz. mushrooms
½ level teaspoon dry mustard	
	1 large onion
for the filling:	1 large cooking apple
1 lb. streaky bacon, roughly chopped	treacle*
	seasoning

*A very unusual but rich flavour is given to this bacon pudding by putting in a small quantity of black treacle. This gives a particularly rich mixture but could be left out completely. The black treacle also provides a certain amount of moisture so if it is not being used, add a little stock or water.

1 Make suet pastry, sieving flour, salt and mustard.
2 Chop bacon, cabbage heart or mushrooms and onion.
3 Peel and dice the apple, add to bacon mixture with the treacle.
4 Line a greased 2½ pint pudding basin with two-thirds of the pastry.
5 Fill with the bacon and vegetable mixture and season to taste.
6 Cover with a lid made from the remaining dough.
7 Cover with greased greaseproof paper or foil. Steam steadily for 3 hours.

To Fry Meat

In most cases, meat to be fried is either tender and young (see tables for each type of meat, page 7) or it is meat made into hamburgers, rissoles, etc. Here are the points to remember:

1 For shallow frying, make certain that the oil or fat is hot before the meat goes in, with the exception of bacon, which goes into a cold pan, see page 52.
2 Seal the meat on either side, then turn down the heat immediately to make absolutely certain that you do not overcook the outside before the centre of the meat is cooked.
3 Drain fried meats well.

Methods of frying meat

Shallow frying

You need just enough oil or fat to cover the bottom of the frying pan when melted and give a depth of about ¼–½ inch, at the most.

The fat or oil should be heated only until a FAINT haze is seen. Fry the meat quickly on either side, then reduce the heat to make sure the meat is cooked right the way through to the middle.

Deep frying

Put the oil or fat into a deep saucepan or proper fryer, and heat until a faint haze is seen or a cube of bread turns golden brown within a minute. Do not get the fat any hotter than this, otherwise the meat will burn.

In order to remove the meat easily it can be put into a frying basket and lowered into the hot oil or fat.

After the outside of the meat is crisped or browned, lower the heat to make sure it cooks through to the centre. Because the meat will be browned on both sides simultaneously, the cooking time can, therefore, be slightly reduced when frying meat in deep fat.

To drain fried meat

1 Lift the meat on to absorbent kitchen paper or crumpled tissue paper, but NOT on to grease-proof paper.
2 Allow to drain for ½ minute and then serve.

To use a frying pan for quick sauces

The frying pan is excellent for making sauce for fried food.

If you are thickening a sauce in the frying pan you need to stir fairly briskly and reduce the heat since the sauce is inclined to cook so quickly that lumps can form.

Simple garnishes with fried meats

Fried potatoes

Raw potatoes, sliced or chip shapes, cooked until golden brown.

Mushrooms

Prepare the mushrooms. Do not skin top-grade ones. Fry gently in shallow fat.

Onions

Cut rings of onion, dip in seasoned flour. Fry in deep or shallow fat. If wished, dip first in milk and then in flour for a thicker coating. For soft fried onions do not coat at all.

Tomatoes

Halve and season the tomatoes. Fry gently in shallow fat until soft.

Maître d'hôtel butter

you will need:

2 oz. butter	1–2 teaspoons
squeeze lemon juice	chopped parsley
	seasoning, optional

1 Work the lemon juice and parsley into the butter.
2 Add seasoning if wished.
3 Form the flavoured butter into a neat shape and chill.
4 Cut into slices and put on any fried or grilled meat.

To fry steak

cooking time: as instructions

Steaks to choose – as for grilling, see page 54

accompaniments:	to garnish:
French or English	tomatoes
mustard	mushrooms
Worcestershire sauce	watercress
	fried onion rings,
	see above

1 Heat a good knob of butter or a little oil in the pan and put the steak in.
2 Fry quickly on either side to seal in the flavour.
3 Lower the heat and cook gently for 10–12 minutes for a well-done steak, 6–8 minutes for a medium steak and 3–4 minutes for an under-done or 'rare' steak.

Tournedos of steak

A fillet steak made into a round is called a tournedos. If you ask the butcher he will tie pieces of fillet steak into neat rounds with string. You need only remove the string before serving. Or simply press the meat with your hands into a circle and then tie it yourself.

The steaks can be fried or grilled.

Each type of garnish gives its name to a tournedos of steak.

Africaine – serve with fried banana and horseradish sauce.

Arlésienne – serve with fried slices of aubergine and tomatoes and topped with rings of fried onion.

Baronne – top with mushrooms and serve with tomato purée and béarnaise sauce, see page 84.

Belle Hélène – serve with asparagus tips and truffles (mushrooms could be substituted).

Calcutta – serve with curry flavoured rice (cook rice, then fry a little curry powder in butter, and toss rice in this), and brown sauce, see page 84, flavoured with chutney.

Carlton – top with chopped egg and serve with béarnaise sauce, see page 84, and strips of cooked tongue, mushrooms and truffle.

Céleri – serve with braised celery.

Chasseur – serve with chasseur sauce, see page 85.

Chéron – serve with artichoke bottoms filled with diced cooked vegetables and topped with béarnaise sauce, see page 84.

Drexel – coat with béarnaise sauce and serve with tomato purée topped with truffle and thin, match-stick potatoes.

Dumas – coat with onion sauce, see page 85, sprinkle with cheese and brown under the grill. Top with slices of ham and serve with potato croquettes.

Majestic – serve on a purée of cooked mushrooms and in a creamed potato border with béarnaise sauce, see page 84.

Ménagère – serve in a border of duchesse potato, topped with tiny pieces of carrot, turnip and onions, and with brown or espagnole sauce, see page 85.

Nesselrode – serve with a well-seasoned purée of chestnuts and fried potatoes.

Niçoise – serve with cooked French beans and tiny tomatoes.

Othello – top with fried or poached egg.

D'Orsay – top with stuffed olives and mushrooms.

Parisienne – top with asparagus tips and béarnaise sauce, see page 84.

Pompadour – top with tomato purée and a slice of grilled or fried ham and truffle (or mushrooms).

Scribe – serve on cooked rice, topped with a little pâté and Madeira sauce, see page 85.

One generally serves a tournedos on a round or large croûton of fried bread. You can dispense with this if you wish but it raises the meat and makes it look more impressive.

Steak Diane

cooking time: few minutes

you will need for 4 servings:

1 very finely chopped onion OR shallot	little Worcestershire sauce
2–3 oz. butter	little brandy, optional
4 very thin slices of sirloin or rump steak*	little chopped parsley

*Fillet steak is rarely used because it is not quite big enough.

1 Fry the onion or shallot in the butter for a minute or two.
2 Add the steak and cook on either side.
3 Lift out on to plates or hot dishes.
4 Add Worcestershire sauce and the brandy to the butter ignite if wished, and pour over the steaks.
5 Garnish with chopped parsley.

Steak au poivre

Brush the steak with plenty of butter and add finely crushed peppercorns to both sides. Grill or fry steadily to personal taste. Lift on to a hot dish, add a little brandy to the butter remaining in the pan. Heat and pour over the steak.

This is very hot and unless people like such a definite flavour, it is better to grill or fry the steak and serve with poivrade sauce, see page 85.

Creole steak

cooking time: 15 minutes

you will need for 4 servings:

1¼ lb. fillet or other steak	seasoning
2 oz. butter	**to serve:**
2 onions	boiled rice or noodles
several sticks celery	
medium can tomatoes and 4 tablespoons beef stock OR 8–12 oz. skinned fresh tomatoes and ¼ pint stock	**to garnish:** chopped parsley

1 Cut the steak into neat fingers, toss in the hot butter with the skinned sliced onions and diced celery.
2 Add the tomatoes and stock, season and simmer for about 10 minutes.
3 Serve in a border of rice or noodles and garnish with chopped parsley.

Hamburgers

cooking time: 25–30 minutes

you will need for 4 servings:

1 lb. minced beef	1 heaped teaspoon chopped parsley
1 large or 2 medium-sized onions	1 teaspoon Worcestershire sauce
seasoning	1 good-sized potato
½ teaspoon mixed herbs	

1 Put meat into a basin.
2 Add grated onion, seasoning, herbs, parsley and sauce.
3 Lastly grate in raw peeled potato.
4 Mix thoroughly together.
5 There will be no need to add liquid as the potato binds the mixture together.

6 Form into large flat cakes and either fry steadily in hot fat or bake on a well-greased tin for about 25–30 minutes in a moderately hot oven (400°F. – Gas Mark 5).
7 The cakes can be floured or tossed in crisp breadcrumbs before cooking; don't try to turn into a neat rissole shape.
8 Serve hot and, if wished, with a fried egg on top.

Baconburgers and curry sauce

cooking time: 20 minutes

you will need for 4 servings:

4 slices bacon	¼ teaspoon garlic salt
1 lb. minced beef	2 tablespoons butter or margarine
⅛ teaspoon pepper	4 slices of toast
½ teaspoon salt	

1 Fry bacon until almost crisp.
2 Remove from pan and quickly curl each strip around the end of a wooden spoon. Secure each with a tooth-pick.
3 Mix together the beef, pepper, salt and garlic salt. Shape into 4 patties and sauté in the butter or margarine for 6 minutes.
4 Put each patty on a slice of toast, top with a bacon curl and pour curry sauce over each.

Curry sauce – make ½ pint white sauce (see page 86), adding 2 teaspoons curry powder and ¼ teaspoon garlic salt.

Scandinavian mixed meat balls

cooking time: 15–20 minutes

you will need for 4 servings:

1 large onion	good pinch sage or thyme
2 oz. butter	
1 egg	
8 oz. minced beef	
salt and pepper	**to garnish:**
1 oz. flour	quartered tomatoes
8 oz. minced pork or veal	mushrooms

1 Peel and finely chop onion.
2 Fry it in butter until soft and golden.
3 Beat the egg. Add half of it to the minced beef,

together with the fried onion, salt, pepper and half the flour.

4 Form the mixture into small balls.

5 Season the minced pork or veal with a good pinch of sage or thyme, salt and pepper.

6 Form this mixture into small balls blending in the remaining egg and flour.

7 Fry these balls in the butter in which the onions were fried.

8 Serve them garnished with fried quartered tomatoes and fried mushrooms.

Variations

Spicy meat balls – use recipe above, but all pork instead of mixture of meats. Omit large onion, but instead fry 2 teaspoons chopped ginger. Season with good pinch sugar and crushed peppercorns, and mix with sherry and soya sauce instead of egg.

Swedish croquettes – use recipe above, but add one tablespoon capers, and same amount of diced beetroot to meat mixture. Form into croquette shapes, coat with well-seasoned flour, then fry.

Viennese steaks – recipe as meat balls, but use all minced beef, season well, add parsley, nutmeg, little tomato ketchup to flavour. Form into flat cakes then fry and top with fried onions.

To fry lamb

Lamb chops or cutlets are ideal for frying.
The difference between a chop and a cutlet is that a cutlet has one long bone running the whole length of the meat, and a chop has a short T-bone. A cutlet is cut from best end of neck and includes a rib. A chop is cut from the loin and includes a section of the backbone.
When lamb cutlets and chops are not coated, they are generally fried in shallow fat.

When a cutlet has been cooked it is correct to decorate it with a cutlet frill. You can buy these in boxes from a good stationers, or make your own.

To coat cutlets or chops

Dip the meat in a little seasoned flour and then in egg and fine breadcrumbs.
Because meat takes an appreciable time to cook it is better, if time permits, to prepare fresh white crumbs rather than use packet or homemade 'raspings' or brown crumbs.
Make sure that you pat the crumbs firmly into the meat, and shake away any surplus which could brown in the fat.
Coated meat can be fried in shallow fat but it is better to use deep fat to give a crisp coating.

Garnishes for cutlets or chops

Both grilled and fried lamb or mutton cutlets and chops can be served with various garnishes which give the name to the dish. Unless stated to the contrary, they can be fried or grilled according to personal taste. Where the word 'coated' occurs, it means that the chops are first brushed with egg and tossed in crumbs before frying.

Aux concombres – serve with rings of peeled fried cucumber.

Duchesse – coat and serve in a border of green peas cooked to a smooth purée. Serve with espagnole sauce, see page 85.

Financière – fry or grill and serve with cooked onions and carrots.

Italienne – marinate in equal quantities of oil and vinegar with plenty of mixed herbs. Drain. Coat, then fry and serve with mushrooms, chopped shallots.

Jardinière – coat and serve with a colourful garnish of mixed spring vegetables.

Maréchal – coat with beaten egg and grated cheese, not crumbs. Serve with bigarade sauce, see page 86. Steam cutlets first for 10 minutes – see below to make sure cheese is not overcooked.

Nelson* (particularly suitable for mutton cutlets) – after steaming spread with a veal stuffing, top with grated cheese and bake in the oven until tender. Serve with a purée of onions.

Réforme – coat, but mix the crumbs with very finely diced bacon or chopped ham. Garnish with cooked strips of ham, mushrooms and hard-boiled egg and serve with poivrade sauce, see page 85. Often one finds strips of beetroot substituted for ham.

***If serving mutton cutlets, it is a very good idea, unless you are sure they are young, to steam the cutlets for about 10 minutes, then coat and fry. In this way you give an attractive appearance and are quite sure that they will be tender.

Scotch cutlets

cooking time: 20–25 minutes

you will need for 4 servings:

4 lamb cutlets	1 egg
a few sprigs mint	breadcrumbs
salt and pepper	
fat for frying	**to garnish:**
1 lb. sausage meat	parsley

1 Thoroughly season the cutlets with chopped mint and a little salt and pepper.
2 Cook them by frying or grilling.
3 When cold, coat each cutlet in sausage meat.
4 Dip in beaten egg and coat with breadcrumbs.
5 Fry in hot deep fat.
6 Serve sprinkled with coarsely chopped parsley.

To fry veal

Veal is admirable for frying. Choose the fillet cuts from the top of the leg. While it is not necessary to have these very thin, the most popular form of fried veal is as an escalope or a Wiener schnitzel and the meat for this is cut very thinly by the butcher. If you decide it is not sufficiently thin, then beat it with a rolling pin to give the required thickness.

Many people feel that the garnish for a good escalope needs to be only a wedge or ring of lemon. You will find more elaborate garnishes opposite, but here are some simple suggestions: Top the escalope with – rings of lemon; freshly chopped hard-boiled egg and parsley; sliced hard-boiled egg and capers.

It is also excellent with green salad.

For a more substantial meal, the fillets of veal can be topped with fried egg and served with tomato sauce, see page 85.

Other ways of frying veal

Veal chops or cutlets can be fried in exactly the same way as lamb or they can be grilled very satisfactorily.

Slices of veal can be fried without coating. This is particularly delicious with thicker pieces of veal.

Escalope of veal or Wiener schnitzel

cooking time: about 8–12 minutes

you will need for 4 servings:

4 thin fillets of veal	1 egg
flour	crumbs for coating*
seasoning	4 oz. butter

*See the comment under Coating lamb chops and cutlets, page 48.

1 Coat the veal with the seasoned flour and then with the egg and crumbs as described under coating lamb.
2 To fry the veal you can use approximately 4 oz. butter or, since butter is inclined to discolour slightly with heating, although it gives a lovely flavour, many people like to use 2 oz. butter and 2 tablespoons oil. You could use a little fat if wished.
3 Heat the butter or butter and oil, put in the fillets of veal, cook fairly quickly on either side until crisp and brown.
4 Lower the heat and cook for a few minutes to make certain the veal, which does need thorough cooking, is tender right through to the middle.

The following are suggestions for garnishes to veal. Cutlets can be grilled or fried.

Cordon bleu – there are two ways of making this dish. *Either* have very large escalopes of veal and cover with a slice of Gruyère cheese and ham. Fold over to make a sandwich, coat and fry longer than usual since the veal will be double thickness.

Or, do not coat the veal, but fry in butter, top with ham and cheese when nearly cooked, and put under the grill.

Cracovienne – garnish cutlets with strips of anchovy fillets and serve with Madeira sauce, see page 85.

Florentine – escalopes or cutlets served on a bed of creamed spinach.

Holstein – garnish with slices of hard-boiled egg, anchovy fillets, gherkins, and capers.

Maître d'hôtel – grill or fry cutlets and top with maître d'hôtel butter, see page 45.

à la maréchale – coated cutlets fried and served with bigarade sauce, see page 86.

à la milanaise – escalopes or cutlets coated with egg and, instead of plain crumbs, an equal quantity of crumbs and Parmesan cheese. Serve with cooked macaroni topped with Parmesan cheese.

Soubise – cutlets of escalopes of veal fried and served with onion purée.

Viennoise – serve with brown sauce, see page 84, with gherkins, olives, capers, fillets of anchovies and hard-boiled egg.

Zingara – fried veal cutlets served on top of cutlet-shaped pieces of grilled or boiled ham and Madeira sauce, see page 85.

Other ways to serve veal fillets or cutlets

Cidered veal – fry the veal in butter, then add enough cider to cover pan, with chopped onion, parsley, seasoning. Simmer gently until meat is cooked.

With macaroni and tomato – this is similar to à la milanaise, except cooked sliced tomatoes and onions are blended with cooked macaroni.

Royal veal – fry veal fillets in plenty of butter, when tender remove to hot dish, fry mushrooms in same pan, then stir wineglass of sherry and same amount of cream into pan, heat, pour over veal, add chopped parsley.

With fruit sauce – fry the veal fillets, meanwhile prepare bigarade (orange) sauce, see page 86. Just before serving add about 2 oz. halved and seeded grapes.

With sour cream – fry the veal fillets, adding mushrooms to the butter. When nearly ready to serve cover with about ½ pint sour cream or fresh cream and little lemon juice, beaten with 2 eggs or egg yolks. Heat gently, then serve at once.

Veal balls

cooking time: 15 minutes

you will need for 4 servings:

1 lb. stewing veal	2 oz. butter or bacon
8 oz. boiled potatoes	fat
(weight when	½ pint soured cream
cooked)	OR ½ pint thin cream
1 medium onion	and 1 tablespoon
seasoning	lemon juice
1 egg	

1 Mince the veal and blend with the mashed potatoes very finely chopped or grated onion, seasoning and egg.
2 Form into small round balls, then flatten slightly.
3 Fry in the butter or bacon fat until golden. Add soured cream or cream and lemon juice, and simmer for about 10 minutes.

Seasoned veal rolls

cooking time: 15 minutes

you will need for 4 servings:

1 small onion	4 oz. butter
4 oz. mushrooms	4 very thinly sliced
2 rashers bacon	veal fillets
1 egg	flour

1 Mince the onion, mushrooms and bacon together.
2 Bind to a spreading consistency with a little beaten egg.
3 Heat half the butter.
4 Put the veal fillets into the butter and fry on one side only for ½ minute, lift out of pan.
5 Spread the cooked side with the onion mixture.
6 Roll the slices and secure with wooden cocktail stick.
7 Roll in flour and add the remaining butter to the pan.
8 Allow the rolls to cook slowly in the frying pan.

To fry pork

It is a good idea to slit the fat of a pork chop or cutlet round the edge at ½-inch intervals to encourage this to crisp.

Do not use deep fat for frying pork. There is generally a good distribution of fat and lean meat and using shallow fat will ensure that the chops or cutlets are not too greasy.

Garnishes to serve with pork chops

Pork chops have a very definite flavour so there is less need for a variety of garnishes.

The following are garnish suggestions.

Aux fines herbes – add a good sprinkling of herbs when grilling the pork chops and season a brown sauce, see page 84, with plenty of herbs.

Indienne – serve fried pork chops with a curry sauce, see page 73, and boiled rice.

Soubise – serve grilled or fried pork chops or cutlets with smooth onion purée.

Pork with cucumber

cooking time: 6 minutes

you will need for 4 servings:

8 oz. fillet of pork	2 tablespoons cooking
½–1 tablespoon soy or	oil
soya sauce	1 cucumber
	¼ teaspoon salt

1 Cut the pork into very narrow fingers and marinate for a time in the soy or soya sauce, turning over until it is thoroughly absorbed.
2 Fry in the hot oil for 3 minutes.
3 Season the thinly sliced cucumber and fry with the pork for a further 3 minutes.

Sweet and sour pork

cooking time: 10 minutes

you will need for 4 servings:

1 medium-sized onion	salt and pepper to
1 clove garlic	taste
2 tart eating apples	1 medium-sized can
1 green pepper	pineapple pieces
1 lb. pork fillet	
1 tablespoon flour	**for frying:**
sweet and sour sauce	oil

1 Chop the onion very finely and cook for a few minutes in boiling, salted water. Drain. It should still be rather nutty.
2 Crush the garlic, mix with the diced apples and green pepper.
3 Cut the pork into tiny strips and roll in the seasoned flour.
4 Toss the garlic mixture in the hot oil, then add the pork and cook for a few minutes.
5 Add the drained pineapple and the onion and continue cooking until tender.
6 Serve with the sweet and sour sauce.

Sweet and sour sauce

cooking time: 10 minutes

you will need:

2 tablespoons vinegar	2–3 oz. chopped
1½ tablespoons sugar	pineapple OR, for a
½ tablespoon tomato	more spicy flavour,
ketchup OR purée	2–3 oz. very finely
1 dessertspoon	chopped mustard
cornflour	pickles
1½ teaspoons soy	2 oz. very finely
sauce	chopped onion,
½ pint water	spring onions or
2 teaspoons oil	pickled onions

1 Blend vinegar, sugar, tomato ketchup, cornflour and soy sauce with the water.
2 Put into a saucepan and cook until thickened.
3 Add the oil and continue cooking for a few minutes.
4 Stir in the pineapple or pickles and onion.

Crispy pork cutlets

cooking time: 20 minutes

you will need for 4 servings:

4 thin pork cutlets	water
1 lb. peas	salt and pepper
2 oz. butter	pinch sugar
lettuce leaves	1 egg white
6–8 tiny onions	breadcrumbs

1 Ask your butcher for thin cutlets – with thick ones the breadcrumbs will be cooked long before the meat.
2 First prepare the peas* by tossing them in 1 oz. butter for a few minutes.
3 Add 3–4 shredded lettuce leaves and the onions.
4 Barely cover with water.
5 Season with salt, pepper and a pinch of sugar, and allow to simmer gently until tender. Drain.
6 Season the pork chops with salt and pepper, coat them with beaten egg white then a thick layer of breadcrumbs.
7 Cook them in butter on both sides until the meat is tenderly cooked and the crumb coating crisp and golden brown.
8 Serve with the peas.

*If you are using canned or frozen peas, they will not require cooking for as long as fresh ones, so cook the onions separately and blend them with the cooked peas and shredded lettuce just before serving.

Pork chops with sage sauce

cooking time: 20 minutes

you will need for 4 servings:

4 loin pork chops	1 oz. flour
1 egg	6 level tablespoons
dry sage and onion	sleved tomato pulp
stuffing*	½ pint stock
2 oz. bacon or pork fat	½ teaspoon sage
or lard	seasoning

*You need approximately half a packet of prepared stuffing or use 2 oz. very fine dried breadcrumbs and a good pinch dried sage.

1 Remove bones from the chops, trim, beat with rolling pin until flattened.
2 Dip in the beaten egg. Toss in stuffing.
3 Fry gently in hot fat on both sides until browned and tender. Place on a hot dish.
4 Add the flour and sieved tomato to the pan, stir while adding stock and when thickened add sage and season well.
5 Pour this sauce round the pork.
6 Serve with crispy fried potatoes and spinach.

Variation

Tipsy pork chops – cook as above, but add ¼ pint red wine instead of tomato pulp.

To fry bacon

Rashers of bacon should be put into a pan as follows:
1 Place the first rasher in, having removed the rind, then lay the lean of the second rasher on top of the fat of the first.
2 Continue filling the cold pan in this way.
3 You then need no extra fat, but are sure that the bacon cooks without sticking to the pan.

In the case of thick back rashers, often known today as 'bacon chops', you also start with a cold pan but will, of course, cook steadily to make sure the thick bacon is cooked through to the middle.

With very lean gammon you may need a little butter or fat in the pan to make sure this is kept really moist.

Deep frying is rarely used for bacon.

Bacon rolls can of course be cooked in a frying pan rather than in the oven.

Make the rolls, see page 56, put them on the skewer, fry steadily on one side, turn over and fry on the other side.

Potato and bacon pancakes

cooking time: 15 minutes

you will need for 4 servings:

1 lb. boiled potatoes	½ pint pancake batter,
4 rashers bacon	see below
2 oz. mushrooms	fat or oil for cooking
1 chopped onion	2 oz. grated Cheddar
	cheese

1 Cut boiled potatoes into small cubes.
2 Cut bacon in small pieces and fry, add mushrooms and onion.
3 When cooked, mix with the potatoes.
4 Meanwhile make pancakes in the usual way, see below.
5 Spoon some of the hot savoury potato mixture on to each one.
6 Sprinkle with grated cheese and roll up.

Basic pancake mixture

cooking time: few minutes

you will need:

4 oz. plain flour	½ pint milk
pinch salt	little fat for frying
1 egg	

1 Sieve flour and salt into a bowl.
2 Make a well in the centre.
3 Beat the egg and add to the flour.
4 Pour in half the milk and mix with a whisk to a smooth batter. Mix well to remove all lumps.
5 Add remaining milk.
6 Strain the batter and allow to stand for 1 hour.
7 Melt a little fat in the pan, using just enough to keep the pancake from sticking.
8 Pour sufficient batter to cover the pan very thinly and fry on one side for approximately 1 minute.
9 Turn or toss over and continue cooking for about ½ minute until pancakes are a golden brown colour.

To fry sausages

Heat a very tiny knob of fat in the frying pan. This makes sure the sausages do not stick before their own fat comes out with frying.

To prevent the sausage bursting while cooking, prick lightly with a fine skewer or a fork. Cook steadily until brown on the under side and turn over.

When thoroughly brown, lower the heat to make sure they are adequately cooked through to the centre.

Sausages can be deep fried, but make certain that the fat is not too hot, for even with pricking they can burst through the skins.

Sausage Sorrento

cooking time: 30 minutes

you will need for 4 servings:

2 oz. fat	2 oz. mushrooms
1 lb. sausages	2 oz. lean ham
6 oz. spaghetti	12 oz. tomatoes
1 medium-sized onion	

1 Melt 1 oz. fat in a frying pan and fry the sausages gently for 20 minutes until evenly browned.
2 Meanwhile cook the spaghetti for 10–15 minutes in boiling salted water.
3 Drain and keep hot.
4 Remove the sausages from the frying pan and keep hot.

5 Melt the remaining 1 oz. of fat in the same pan and fry the chopped onion and mushrooms gently for 2–3 minutes.
6 Add the diced ham and lastly the skinned and chopped tomatoes.
7 Season and heat through.
8 Place the spaghetti on a serving dish, pour the tomato mixture over and lay the sausages on top.

Ways to serve sausages

Sausages in batter – see Toad-in-the-hole page 37. Substitute 1 lb. sausages for the meat – heat sausages first before adding the batter.

Sausage croquettes – add finely diced bacon and chopped parsley to sausage meat, form into croquettes. Coat with egg and crumbs and fry.

Sausage risotto – add fried sliced sausages, diced fried bacon and mushrooms to cooked rice, season well.

Tomato croquettes – blend sausage meat with sieved tomato purée, finely chopped chives or onion, coat with egg and crumbs and fry.

To Grill Meat

The meat you choose for grilling MUST be really prime. It is impossible to try to grill inferior quality meat which would be perfectly all right in a casserole or a stew. Here are points to remember when grilling meat:

1 With the exception of bacon, see page 56, the grill must always be pre-heated before the meat is put underneath. By doing this you ensure that the outside of the meat is seared, and the flavour enclosed in the shortest possible time.
2 Keep lean meat well basted with either oil, melted butter or fat, so there is no chance for it to become hard and dry on the outside.
3 Because grilling is a quick method of cooking, do not leave the meat untended for any length of time. Turn it carefully.
4 When turning meat, use either two knives or special tongs. If you insert a fork into a piece of partially cooked meat, you allow the juice to escape and so lose some of the essential flavour.
5 For full details of grilling each type of meat, see under their separate headings.

To line a grill pan with foil

A grill pan is quite difficult to clean and if you line the base of the grill pan with a little foil, and put this over the grid as well, you keep in all the juices and the pan needs only a wipe afterwards.

To brown under the grill

Besides the recipes given in this chapter, you will find grilling most suitable for giving added crispness to certain cooked meats. Just put under the grill for a few minutes.

To use an infra-red grill

An infra-red grill cooks meat extremely quickly. Follow the manufacturer's directions implicitly and do not try to cut down on the pre-heating time. In order to get the very best result it is important that pieces of meat are of even thickness so it can be evenly cooked.

Garnishes for grilled meats

Grilled mushrooms and tomatoes can be cooked at the same time as the grilled meats.

The construction of grill pans varies a little. Where you have a fairly open wire grid, the meat can be put on this and the vegetables, topped with a little butter and seasoning, will cook at the same time underneath and be basted by the fat dropping from the meat.

Where you have a fairly solid grid in a grill pan, you must either put the vegetables on the grid with the meat and keep them very well brushed with melted fat so they do not burn, or you must commence cooking in the base of the grill pan, then put the meat on top and the vegetables will have finished cooking by the time the meat is ready.

Kebabs

This dish of skewered meat has become a favourite. Cubes of meat, lamb, mutton, beef, pork or veal are threaded on metal skewers alternately with slices of aubergine, rings of onion, small mushrooms, little tomatoes, and they are cooked steadily under the grill. Rest skewers on the grill pan if possible, so any surplus fat drops through into the pan. Brush very well with melted fat, butter or oil before cooking and keep well basted during cooking.

Mixed grill

A mixed grill generally consists of a selection of the following: steak, small chop or cutlet, liver, lamb's or pig's kidneys, bacon, sausages, tomatoes, mushrooms, fried egg may be added.

The method of cooking is not difficult. Decide which food needs the longest cooking and start with that on the grill pan. Then gradually add the other foods, depending on their cooking time, so that they will be ready together.

The grill pan will probably not be large enough to hold all the foods necessary, in which case the sausages, tomatoes, and mushrooms can be cooked in the oven, or cooked on the grill first, and then kept hot. Do not cook those foods that dry out easily – steaks, liver, kidneys – first and then keep them hot.

To grill beef steak

cooking time: underdone or 'rare': 4–6 minutes
medium: 9–12 minutes
well-done: 10–15 minutes

Steaks to choose – see below.

1 Make sure the grill is really hot before the steak is put underneath.
2 Brush the grid of the grill and the steak with plenty of oil or butter.
3 For an underdone or rare steak, cook quickly on either side for 2–3 minutes.

For a medium steak, lower the heat and cook for a further 5–6 minutes.

For a well-done steak, lower the heat as much as possible and cook very gently so that it will cook right through to the centre without scorching on the outside.

Steaks can be served with any of the following: grilled mushrooms, grilled tomatoes, fried onions, rings of lemon and capers, crisp green salad, béarnaise sauce, see page 84.

For more elaborate garnishes see Tournedos, page 46.

Steaks to choose for grilling

Minute steak – very thin slice of steak which only needs cooking for 1 minute on either side.

Rump steak – not so tender as fillet steak, but full of flavour.

Fillet steak – lean, very tender steak.

Sirloin steak – a cut from across the sirloin which is well balanced in fat and lean.

Entrecôte – tender, good flavour. Cut from middle ribs or sirloin.

Point steak – cut from pointed end of rump. Most tender.

Porterhouse – very large sirloin steak – up to 4 lb.

Planked steak – the steak is cooked and served on a special wooden board of well-seasoned hardwood. The board is heated in the oven and oiled before the meat is put on it. Grill the meat at a safe distance from the heat.

Tournedos – pieces of fillet steak tied into a circle with a string, served with various garnishes.

Garrick steak

cooking time: 20 minutes

you will need for 4 servings:

1 shallot or 1 teaspoon onion, finely chopped	1–1½ lb. rump steak cut thickly (about 1½ inches)
½ oz. butter	salad oil
4 oz. mushrooms	
1 teaspoon chopped parsley	**for the sauce:**
1 teaspoon thyme	½ oz. butter
1 oz. chopped ham	1 teaspoon chopped parsley
1 tablespoon fresh breadcrumbs	dash Worcestershire sauce OR squeeze lemon juice
seasoning	

1 Soften the chopped shallot or onion in the butter.
2 Wash the mushrooms in salted water. Chop finely and add to the pan with the herbs.
3 Cover and cook 5–7 minutes.
4 Draw aside. Add ham, crumbs, and seasoning. Turn out to cool.
5 Cut the steak on one side to form a pocket. Fill with the stuffing and sew up with thread.
6 Brush the steak with a little salad oil and grill 4–5 minutes on each side.
7 Remove the thread before serving.
8 Melt the butter and when light brown add the parsley and the Worcestershire sauce or lemon juice and pour over the steak.

Carpet bag steak

In this excellent dish which was created in Australia, thick steaks are split and filled with seasoned oysters, and the opening is then sewn with thread before cooking.

Rump steak Melbourne

Grill the rump steak, and garnish with tomatoes and mushrooms. Serve with parsley butter.

To grill chops and cutlets

A mutton chop or cutlet will probably be more tender if it is steamed for about 10 minutes before being put under the grill.
Most lamb or mutton cutlets contain a fairly generous amount of fat and this tends to baste the lean. You can brush the lean part only with a small amount of fat before grilling.

Serve with the same garnishes as fried chops and cutlets, see page 48.

New ways to serve grilled chops

Cheese chops – blend grated cheese with fine breadcrumbs. Brush chops with beaten egg, coat in the cheese crumb mixture then brush with melted butter and grill.

Golden chops – grill chops in usual way on one side, turn, coat uncooked side with finely chopped mushrooms and plenty of grated cheese, brush with butter, grill.

With orange – sprinkle a little orange juice over nearly cooked chops, garnish with orange slices.

Saffron steaks of lamb

cooking time: 20–25 minutes

you will need for 4–6 servings:

½ teaspoon saffron	1 teaspoon fresh ground black pepper
½ pint thick cream	
juice of 1 lemon	1 clove garlic, grated (optional)
2 lb. lamb from shoulder or leg	oil
2 onions, grated	1¼ teaspoons salt

1 Infuse the saffron in a little hot water and mix with the cream and lemon juice.
2 Cut the lamb into individual steak sizes. Rub with grated onion, black pepper and garlic. Cover with the cream and saffron mixture, rubbing well into the meat with the back of a serving spoon.
3 Leave the meat for at least an hour so that it will absorb the spices. (It has a better flavour if left overnight.)
4 Heat the grill and put a little oil into it to prevent the meat sticking. Place the lamb steaks with the marinade sauce under the grill. Cook under a medium heat and turn once to brown both sides. Sprinkle with a little salt before serving.

To grill veal

Because veal is a dry and very lean meat, you must keep it well basted by brushing with melted butter or oil on both sides and during cooking.
Serve with the same garnishes and accompaniments as fried veal, see page 49.

To grill pork

The fat should be crisp and it is helpful to snip this at ½-inch intervals. Keep the lean basted with a little fat during cooking, which has to be fairly prolonged.

Spare rib chops with almonds

cooking time: 10–15 minutes

you will need for 4 servings:

1 tablespoon mustard	4 spare rib pork chops
1 tablespoon brown sugar	1 oz. shredded almonds
	salt and pepper

1 Mix the mustard and sugar and rub over the chops and grill until tender.
2 Sprinkle the almonds over the pork and season with salt and pepper.
3 Return to the grill to brown the almonds.
4 Serve with fried potatoes.

To grill bacon

This is the only meat to put under a grill that has not been pre-heated. Remove rind, snip the edge of the fat, and with gammon, brush the lean with melted butter as it cooks. Thin bacon need not be turned to cook. Serve with the same garnishes and accompaniments as fried bacon, see page 52.

Bacon rolls can be put on a metal skewer and grilled. Balance the skewers on the grid or in the grill pan, and turn as they brown.

Grilled gammon with peaches

cooking time: 12 minutes

you will need for 4 servings:

4 thick slices gammon	2 oz. butter or margarine
4 teaspoons brown sugar	4 half peaches
1 teaspoon dry mustard	little extra brown sugar

1 Cut the rind from the gammon and snip along the edge of the fat to prevent it curling.
2 Mix brown sugar and mustard with butter or margarine and heat gently until the fat has melted.
3 Place the ham on the grill grid and brush with half the fat mixture.
4 Grill for 5–6 minutes, turn and brush with the rest of the mixture.
5 Drain the peaches well and fill the centre of each with brown sugar.
6 Place on the grid by the side of the ham and grill both for a further 5–6 minutes.

Variation

With prunes – use soaked, lightly cooked prunes instead of peaches, sprinkle these with cheese.

To grill sausages

Prick and put on the grid of the grill pan. Turn with tongs so they brown evenly under a hot grill.

Serve with bacon and egg, or as a main dish with vegetables.

To Casserole and Braise

In this chapter the recipes are primarily designed to give the best results with the cheaper cuts of meat. There are certain basic rules to remember when using these comparatively slow methods of cooking.

1 If you shorten the cooking time and increase the heat you will toughen the meat and no matter how long you cook it afterwards, it will never become really tender.
2 On the other hand, do not make the mistake of thinking it does not matter how long the meat is cooked. If you over-cook badly in a stew or

casserole, the meat simply becomes a rather flavourless collection of meat fibres instead of tender, moist meat.

3 If adding vegetables, remember these are designed to make the meat go further as well as adding flavour; that is why you can often allow a smaller serving of meat in a stew or casserole than you can for roasting.
4 In the same way dumplings help to make the meat go further.
5 If you wish your vegetables to retain their full flavour, it is advisable to put in only a few at the

beginning of cooking, then add the remaining vegetables later. This is particularly important when cooking a large piece of meat.

Bouquet garni

In many recipes for savoury casseroles and stews, you often find that a *bouquet garni* is used. This is a small bunch of fresh herbs. Those generally used are parsley, sage, thyme and marjoram and maybe one or two of the less usual herbs, see page 13. Tie these together with cotton and put them in the stew or casserole while it is cooking. Remove before serving.

If you have no fresh herbs, a small teaspoon mixed dried herbs could be used though dried herbs give a rather musty taste if used in excess.

To pressure cook meat

Undoubtedly a pressure cooker is ideal to save time. Any of the recipes for casseroles, stews and braising can be cooked in a pressure cooker. You will find definite timings in your own manufacturer's instruction book. As a general rule, you allow approximately 15 lb. pressure.

beef   – approximately 25 minutes
lamb and mutton – approximately 20 minutes
veal and pork   – approximately 25 minutes

If the recipe requires the liquid to be thickened first many people find, particularly if the base of the pressure cooker is rather thin, that it is advisable to thicken after cooking as in a stew.

The general procedure of using a pressure cooker for these types of dishes is as follows:

1 If the recipe requires the ingredients to be fried first, they are fried on the bottom of the pressure cooker, as if it were an ordinary pan.
2 The liquid is then added, *but because there is no loss of liquid by evaporation, one generally uses approximately half to two-thirds only of the amount given in the recipe.*
3 Add seasoning but be sparing because the mineral salts and full flavours are retained in pressure cooking.
4 Put on the lid – one does not use a rack in casserole dishes.
5 Bring to pressure and allow to cook for the time given.
6 Allow the pressure to drop to room temperature.
7 Remove the lid, add thickening and treat the pressure cooker as an ordinary saucepan as this thickens.

Dumplings

Most people enjoy dumplings in a stew or casserole, and they make a more substantial dish. Here are the important points to remember.

1 The liquid must be boiling fairly steadily when the dumplings go in.
2 The dumplings can be cooked either in the oven, see Gammon slipper and dumplings. page 61, or they can be added to the liquid in a saucepan.
3 Great care must be taken, particularly when adding to a stew in a saucepan, that the liquid really is sufficient. The suet dumpling mixture absorbs quite a lot, and it will be very easy for the stew or braised meat dish to burn at the bottom of the pan.
4 Always add a little extra liquid, if you are not sure that you have sufficient.
5 If adding dumplings to a stew that has to be thickened at the end, remember that dumplings also add a certain amount of thickening, and you can therefore reduce the amount of flour or cornflour in thickening the liquid.
6 Never make the dumplings too big. They will generally swell up to approximately twice their original size, and they look more appetising if they are kept reasonably small.

You will find a recipe for dumplings under Gammon slipper and dumplings, page 61.

Bacon dumplings – add pinch curry powder and about 3 oz. diced and fried cooked bacon to flour.

Celery dumplings – add celery salt to flour, and about 2 tablespoons finely chopped raw celery.

Herb dumplings – add to flour, 2–4 teaspoons chopped fresh herbs or $\frac{1}{2}$–1 teaspoon dried herbs (use all one herb – parsley, chives, or mixed herbs.)

Sausage meat dumplings – use only half quantities of flour, etc., see page 61, then blend with 4 oz. sausage meat.

To casserole meat

If it is more convenient to cook the casserole ingredients in a saucepan you can do so, instead of putting them in a casserole and cooking in the oven. If you are using exactly the same recipe in a saucepan it would be advisable to use just a little more liquid, due to the fact that a certain amount will evaporate during cooking. The evaporation in a casserole should be very small if the lid fits closely. If you are doubtful whether the lid really does fit as well as it might, then cover closely with foil.

Points to remember

1 When you add vegetables they tend to make a little juice of their own as they cook.
2 As a casserole has a fitting lid, which limits evaporation, it is not necessary to make too thin a sauce. The richness of the finished dish is spoiled if the sauce is too thin.
3 Allow plenty of time to cook a casserole, otherwise if you try to hurry it, the meat, unless of very prime quality, will not be as tender as one would wish.
4 If you choose an attractive casserole dish, it is possible to cook and serve in the same container.
5 Use the recipes in this section as ideas, and when you have made them as directed, you can then substitute other flavourings like some of the rather unusual herbs, see page 13.
6 Use spring onions instead of ordinary onions, and red and green peppers as well as tomatoes.
7 Use a little wine, even if not given in the recipe, in place of some of the stock or water. Wine added to meat dishes not only gives a good flavour, but helps to tenderize the meat.

Beef casserole

cooking time: 2½ hours

you will need for 4 servings:

1 lb. beef, flank	1 level teaspoon made
2 rashers streaky	mustard
bacon	¼ pint stock or water,
seasoning	or use canned
1 oz. flour	tomato juice
1 oz. lard or dripping	3–4 tablespoons
or 1 tablespoon	cooked peas or
cooking oil	sweet corn
4 small carrots	4–6 pickled onions
3–4 medium-sized	
potatoes	

1 Dice meat and bacon.
2 Add seasoning to flour. Toss the meat and bacon in flour.
3 Heat fat or oil in a pan, add meat and bacon and fry briskly until brown.
4 Transfer to casserole then add carrots, potatoes, mustard, stock or water. Season.
5 Cover casserole tightly with lid then cook in the centre of a very moderate oven (350°F. – Gas Mark 3) for 1½–2 hours.
6 Add peas or sweet corn and the pickled onions.
7 Cook for a further ½ hour or till meat is tender.
8 Alternatively, the ingredients can be simmered gently for 1½–2 hours in a covered pan on top of the cooker.

Variations

Beef and orange casserole – use cider for liquid, omitting stock. Add juice and finely grated rind of two oranges to the meat, omit potatoes, peas, and pickled onions.

Spiced beef – flavour with little red wine, pinch powdered cloves and plenty of mustard.

Creamy beef casserole – recipe as beef casserole, but use rather less stock, just before serving stir in about ¼ pint thin cream or top of the milk.

Spanish casserole – add good pinch paprika and curry powder to other seasonings. Omit potatoes and use diced green pepper and mushrooms instead.

Cheese-topped casserole – use beef casserole recipe, or any of the variations. Just before serving cover with grated cheese and crumbs and brown under hot grill.

Beef olives

cooking time: 1½–2 hours

you will need for 4 servings:

veal stuffing, see page 28 ¾ pint thin brown sauce, see page 84
1–1¼ lb. stewing steak, cut into 4 thin slices bay leaf
2 oz. dripping or fat

1 Divide stuffing between the pieces of meat and spread over.
2 Form into rolls, or, if the pieces of meat are sufficiently large, gather up into a dumpling shape and secure with thin string or cotton.
3 Heat the dripping in a pan and fry the olives in this until just brown on the outside.
4 Cover with brown sauce, add the bay leaf.
5 Put a lid on the saucepan and simmer gently for 1½ hours, or put into a covered casserole for 2 hours in a very moderate oven (350°F. – Gas Mark 3).
6 Serve with a border of mashed potato and mixed vegetables, cut into small dice before cooking.

Variation

Tomato beef olives – make stuffing using 2 chopped onions, fried in a little fat, and blended with 3 oz. breadcrumbs, 2 skinned chopped tomatoes, 1 tablespoon chopped parsley and seasoning. Serve with tomato sauce and noodles.

Flemish beef

cooking time: about 2 hours

you will need for 4 servings:

1 oz. fat
1½ lb. stewing steak
2 medium-sized onions
2 oz. mushrooms
2 oz. flour
½ pint pale ale, or pale ale and water

1 bay leaf
2 peppercorns
½ level teaspoon mixed herbs
½ level teaspoon marjoram seasoning
1 level teaspoon French mustard
} tied in muslin for a *bouquet garni*

1 Melt the fat in a medium-sized saucepan.
2 Add the meat, cut into 1-inch cubes, fry for 2–3 minutes, until browned on all sides.
3 Add the peeled and sliced onions and mushrooms and fry for a further 2–3 minutes, without allowing them to brown.

4 Sprinkle in the flour, cook for 1–2 minutes, add the pale ale or pale ale and water.
5 Bring to the boil, stirring all the time, and add the *bouquet garni*, seasoning and mustard.
6 When the beef has boiled, transfer it to a 1½ pint casserole, cover with the lid and place in the centre of a very moderate oven (350°F. – Gas Mark 3) for 2 hours.
7 Serve with boiled potatoes.

Chuck steak and mushroom casserole

cooking time: 2 hours

you will need for 4 servings:

4 chuck steaks, 4–6 oz. each
1 oz. flour
salt and pepper

8 oz. thinly sliced onion
4 oz. mushrooms
1 beef extract cube
¼ pint hot water

1 Ask your butcher for steaks cut 1 inch thick.
2 Roll the steak in seasoned flour.
3 Put the sliced onions and mushrooms into a casserole.
4 Place the steaks on top.
5 Dissolve the beef extract cube in hot water.
6 Pour over the steaks.
7 Cover the casserole with foil or the lid.
8 Cook in a slow oven (300°F. – Gas Mark 2) for 2 hours.

Lamb casserole

cooking time: 2–2¼ hours

you will need for 4 servings:

1¼ lb. boned shoulder lamb
2 medium-sized onions
1 large apple

4 oz. plumped, stoned prunes
salt and pepper
¼ pint stock or water*
¼ pint red wine, optional*

1 Cut meat into neat pieces.
2 Peel and slice onions and apple.
3 Place meat in casserole with alternate layers of onion, apple and prunes.
4 Season meat and onion layers well with salt and freshly ground pepper.
5 Add sufficient liquid to come halfway up

casserole, as ingredients will produce a lot of their own juice.

6 Cover casserole and cook in slow oven (300°F. – Gas Mark 2) for 2–2¼ hours.

*If not using red wine, increase the amount of stock or water, but see point 5

Variations

Lamb and butter bean casserole – use the recipe above, but add tomatoes instead of prunes, use all water and omit the wine. Just before ready to serve stir in can of butter beans or about 6 oz. cooked butter beans.

Lamb and broad bean casserole – use a can of broad beans instead of butter beans.

Lancashire hot pot (1)

cooking time: 2 hours

you will need for 4 servings:

1½ lb. potatoes	1 large onion
1–1½ lb. scrag end mutton	1 teaspoon salt
	½ teaspoon pepper
2 sheep's kidneys, optional	¼ pint stock or water

1 Arrange a layer of potatoes at the bottom of the casserole.
2 Cut the meat into pieces and remove the fat from the kidneys, then skin, core and slice them. Place over the potatoes.
3 Add the sliced onion with salt, pepper and stock.
4 Cover with the remainder of the sliced potatoes, and a lid or foil.
5 Bake in a moderate oven (375°F. – Gas Mark 4) for 2 hours, but remove the covering lid or foil for the last 15 minutes.

Lancashire hot pot (2)

Use recipe 1, but omit the kidneys and use two or three onions.

You can add one or two sliced fresh tomatoes with the sliced onion, in place of canned ones.

To encourage the top layer of potatoes to become very crisp, brush with a little melted fat when the lid has been removed.

Veal and anchovy casserole

cooking time: 1¼ hours

you will need for 4 servings:

for the sauce:	
2 anchovies	1 onion
4 oz. tuna or herring, in oil	2 cloves
	1–2 sliced carrots
juice 1 large lemon	1 stick celery
2 tablespoons capers	1 bay leaf
	salt

1¼ lb. fillet of veal	**to garnish:**
6–8 canned anchovy fillets	slices of lemon

1 Make the sauce by washing and boning the anchovies and pounding in a mortar with the tuna fish or herring.
2 Gradually add the fish oil and the lemon juice.
3 The sauce should be rather liquid and there should be enough to cover the meat. Cover the meat with the sauce.
4 Sprinkle the capers over, and allow to stand overnight. Remove the veal.
5 Cut the veal into long neat slices.
6 Cut anchovy into thin strips, thread through the veal with a larding needle and tie up with string OR put one on each slice.
7 Put the meat, the onion stuck with cloves, carrots, chopped celery, bay leaf and a good pinch of salt in a deep pan with enough water to barely cover the meat.
8 Bring this to the boil, simmer for 1¼ hours, then lift meat and vegetables out and arrange on a hot dish.
9 Cover with the sauce and garnish with slices of lemon.

Boston casserole

cooking time: 2–2½ hours

you will need for 4 servings:

1½ lb. hand or belly of pork	1 large onion
	2–3 tomatoes
1 level teaspoon flour	1 medium-sized can baked beans
½ teaspoon salt	
good shake pepper	2 teaspoons brown sugar
1 teaspoon mustard	
little fat	seasoning
4 potatoes	¼ pint stock or water, optional
1 good-sized cooking apple	

1 Dice meat and roll in flour mixed with salt, pepper and mustard.

2 Cook pork steadily, in a pan, with fat until golden brown on the outside.

3 Slice potatoes, peeled apple and onion thinly.

4 Arrange half of these at the bottom of a casserole, seasoning well.

5 Mix the meat with sliced tomatoes, beans and sugar.

6 Put over the layer of potatoes.

7 Cover with remaining onion, apple, then potatoes and season.

8 For a more moist mixture ¼ pint stock or water may be added to the beans.

9 Put lid on casserole and cook in very moderate oven (300–350°F. – Gas Mark 2–3) for 2–2½ hours.

10 Serve with crisp salad or green vegetables.

Bacon and bean casserole

cooking time: 2–2½ hours

you will need for 6 servings:

8 oz. dried butter beans	1 onion
1½ lb. forehock bacon	2 carrots
4 tomatoes	½–1 pint stock or
2 green peppers (capsicums), optional	water with bouillon cube
1 stick celery	seasoning

1 Soak the butter beans overnight in water.

2 Strain off the water.

3 Cut the bacon into chunks.

4 Slice the tomatoes and seeded peppers.

5 Chop the celery, onion and carrots.

6 Place all ingredients into a large casserole and season well.

7 Add the stock, and cover tightly.

8 Cook for 2–2½ hours in a very moderate oven (325°F. – Gas Mark 3) or on a very low setting for 4–5 hours.

9 This casserole is delicious served with jacket potatoes.

Variation

Casserole of beans and peas – use either dried peas instead of dried beans in recipe above, or add fresh peas about ½–¾ hour before serving.

Gammon slipper and dumplings

cooking time: 1 hour 20 minutes

you will need for 6 servings:

1 gammon slipper, about 2 lb.	**for the dumplings:**
2 sliced onions or leeks	4 oz. flour (with plain flour use 1 teaspoon baking powder)
1 14-oz. can tomatoes	1½–2 oz. shredded suet
ground black pepper	salt
1 teaspoon basil	pepper
	water or milk to mix

1 Soak the gammon slipper in cold water, 6 hours if smoked, 2 hours if unsmoked.

2 Place in a casserole, cover with onions or leeks and tomatoes.

3 Season with pepper and basil.

4 Cover tightly and cook for about one hour in a very moderate oven (350°F. – Gas Mark 3), or in saucepan.

5 Mix ingredients for dumplings and divide the dough into eight portions.

6 Remove skin from gammon and place the dumplings in the liquid.

7 Put in the oven with lid on for further 20 minutes, or on top of cooker.

8 Serve with a green vegetable.

Pork sausage casserole

cooking time: 1½ hours

you will need for 4 servings:

4 pork loin chops	1 pint stock or water
3 oz. liver sausage	and stock cube
1 oz. fat	1 oz. flour, optional
½ cabbage	seasoning
3 sliced onions	

1 Spread the chops with liver sausage on one side.

2 Sandwich the liver sausage sides of the chops together and tie firmly.

3 Seal in hot fat and place in a casserole.

4 Shred the cabbage and add this and the onion to the casserole.

5 Pour in the seasoned stock, cover and bake in moderate oven (375°F. – Gas Mark 4) for 1½ hours.

6 Dish up vegetables.

7 Cut the thread of the chops and lay them on top of the vegetables.

8 Thicken the gravy a little with flour, if liked, and pour this over the completed dish.

To braise meat

Braising is a method used in cooking meat and often vegetables, and it is really a combination of roasting or frying and stewing or casseroling. The food is browned first in a little hot fat or oil to seal the outside. A thick sauce is then made with the fat remaining in the pan, flour and a brown stock, and the meat or vegetables replaced in this and then simmered gently. Instead the food can be coated in flour, so adding thickening to the fat as it is fried, an example being Braised beef, see below.

Points to remember

1 A braised meat dish should be reasonably rich, so do not cut down on the amount of fat in any way.
2 You should have a sufficiently thick sauce to absorb this fattiness, because it should never look greasy and unattractive.
3 A braised meat dish can be cooked either in the oven or in a saucepan.
4 Check that the lid of the pan fits very tightly, so the liquid does not evaporate. Put a piece of foil under the lid or add just a little extra stock.
5 Stir once or twice in a saucepan during cooking, but this of course is not necessary when you have the mixture in a casserole.

Braised beef and carrots

cooking time: 2 hours 40 minutes *or*
              3 hours 10 minutes

you will need for 4 servings:

1–1½ lb. stewing beef	2 oz. fat
2 good-sized onions	1 pint brown stock or
8 medium-sized	water with stock
carrots	cube
1 oz. flour	pinch mixed herbs,
seasoning	optional

1 Cut the meat into meat dice.
2 Slice the onions or you can have small onions and leave them whole.
3 Leave the carrots whole, or cut into slices or fingers.
4 Toss the meat in the seasoned flour, and fry in hot fat until golden on the outside.
5 If cooking in a casserole, lift out the meat, and toss the onions and carrots in any fat remaining.
6 If you are cooking in the saucepan, you can add the onions and carrots to the beef and just seal in the hot fat.
7 Gradually stir in the liquid. Add herbs.
8 Bring to the boil, and cook until a smooth thin sauce.
9 Either transfer to a covered casserole and bake for 2½–3 hours in a slow to very moderate oven (300–350°F. – Gas Mark 2–3) or lower the heat and cover the saucepan tightly and cook for approximately 2½ hours.

Variations

Stuffed braised beef – buy the beef in one rather thick slice, split part of the way through the middle to form a 'pocket', put in stuffing – using the flavour you prefer. Tie or skewer tightly and cook as above.
Tomato braised beef – use half tomato juice or thin purée instead of all stock. Add finely diced celery to carrots.
Burgundy beef – use half cheap red wine, and half stock. Add plenty of herbs to flavour.
Polish beef – omit carrots from Braised beef recipe, use about 4 oz. mushrooms instead, together with 2–3 rashers diced bacon. Flavour with 2 tablespoons vinegar. Serve with parsley flavoured dumplings.
Jugged beef – omit carrots and flavour with grated lemon rind and plenty of herbs. Keep onions whole and remove before serving beef.

Cassoulet

cooking time: 5 hours

you will need for 7–8 servings:

1 lb. haricot beans	1 crushed clove garlic
1 ham bone	6 small onions
1 oz. brown sugar	2 tablespoons tomato
1 tablespoon black	purée
treacle	*bouquet garni*
2 pints stock	salt and pepper
2 oz. dripping	3 frankfurter sausages
1 lb. belly	white breadcrumbs
pork ⎱ cut into	
1 lb. stewing ⎱ small	
mutton or ⎱ pieces	
lamb ⎭	

1 Soak the beans in cold water overnight.
2 Drain and put them in a saucepan with the ham bone, sugar and treacle.

3 Cover with the stock and simmer for two hours.

4 Melt the dripping and lightly brown the diced meat, then add the garlic, onions, tomato purée, *bouquet garni* and seasoning.

5 Cook gently for a few minutes.

6 Drain the beans and keep the stock.

7 Put a layer of beans in a deep casserole, then add the meat mixture, then beans and meat alternately, ending with the beans.

8 Just cover with some of the stock and cook in centre of slow oven (300°F. – Gas Mark 2) for 3 hours. Add more liquid if needed.

9 One hour before serving add the sausages cut up, cover with breadcrumbs and continue cooking but without lid.

Chilli con carne

cooking time: 55 minutes–1½ hours

you will need for 4 servings:

2 oz. butter or margarine	12 oz.–1 lb. minced beef or diced beef
1 large onion	8 oz. tomatoes OR
1 green pepper	1 pint tomato pulp
2 sticks celery	8 oz. cooked kidney
1 tablespoon chilli powder*	beans or soaked and cooked haricot
½ teaspoon salt	beans
cayenne pepper	¼ pint water
2 teaspoons paprika pepper	

*This is correct, but see note, page 16

1 Heat the margarine in a saucepan.

2 Chop the onion, pepper and celery, cook in the margarine until just tender, then add the other ingredients.

3 Bring just to the boil, lower the heat and cook gently for approximately 55 minutes or 1½ hours if diced meat is used.

4 Stir halfway through the cooking, and add a little more water if necessary.

5 Some people like to add 2 oz. cooked rice to the recipe.

Variation

Bacon con carne – diced forehock or rather thick rashers of bacon can be used in place of beef in Chilli con carne. Use rather less salt in the recipe.

Braised lamb cutlets

cooking time: 1¼ hours

you will need for 4 servings:

4 large or 8 small lamb cutlets	2 teaspoons chopped parsley
1½ oz. butter	2 tablespoons wine vinegar
4 onions	salt and pepper
8 oz. tomatoes	little water

1 Brown the cutlets on both sides in the butter.

2 Remove from the pan, slice the onions and stir well into the butter.

3 Add the skinned sliced tomatoes, parsley, vinegar and seasoning.

4 Place the cutlets on top of the vegetables and pour in a little water.

5 Cover the pan and cook gently for 1 hour.

Porcstronni

cooking time: 1 hour 5 minutes

you will need for 2 servings:

8 oz. lean belly of pork	½ clove garlic, optional
1 small red pepper	1 meat cube
1 carrot	1 pint water
1 small onion	2 oz. cut spaghetti
1 oz. bacon fat	parsley for garnish

1 Cut meat into 1-inch dice. Halve the pepper and remove the seeds.

2 Slice pepper finely, together with the carrot and onion.

3 Heat the bacon fat and toss vegetables in this.

4 Add crushed garlic, if liked, and the meat.

5 Dissolve meat cube in water, add to the meat.

6 Simmer for about 50 minutes. Skim off fat.

7 Add the spaghetti. Cook for a further 15 minutes.

8 Serve in deep bowls garnished with chopped parsley.

9 If using long spaghetti break into 1½–2 inch lengths.

10 If doubling the portions try to use one red pepper and one green pepper.

Variation

Pork and caper sauce – pork can be served with caper sauce in the same way as lamb, see recipe on page 71.

Veal marengo

cooking time: 1 hour 10 minutes

you will need for 4 servings:

1 lb. neck veal	½ pint white stock **or**
flour	water
seasoning	8 oz. skinned tomatoes
3 oz. butter or 3	2 oz. mushrooms
tablespoons oil	4 slices bread
2 finely chopped	butter or oil for frying
onions or shallots	parsley
	lemon

1 Cut the meat into neat pieces, coat with a thin layer of seasoned flour.
2 Fry until pale golden brown in the hot butter or oil.
3 Add finely chopped onions and fry until transparent.
4 Add stock, chopped tomatoes and mushrooms.
5 Season well.
6 Simmer gently for approximately 1 hour.
7 Serve garnished with croûtons of fried bread, parsley and lemon slices.

Variation

With wine – for special occasions, use half water and half white wine instead of stock.

Pork ratatouille

cooking time: 1 hour

you will need for 4 servings:

2 oz. lard	3 chopped mushrooms
2 sliced onions	1 lb. diced shoulder of
1 clove garlic or pinch	pork
garlic salt	salt and pepper
2 green peppers	1 tablespoon
about 1 lb. young	concentrated
marrow	tomato purée
	¼ pint stock

1 Melt the lard and fry the onions and crushed garlic in saucepan.
2 Seed and chop the peppers.
3 Wash and cut up unskinned marrow into small pieces and add these, with the mushrooms and pork, to the pan.
4 Stir well and season to taste.
5 Mix the tomato purée with the stock and add to the pan.
6 Cover with lid and simmer gently for 1 hour.
7 This dish can also be cooked slowly in the oven at 350°F. – Gas Mark 3 for 1¼ hours.

Cream pork fricassée

cooking time: 2¾ hours

you will need for 4 servings:

1½ lb. neck pork	1 oz. flour
¾ pint white wine	salt
4 small onions	¼ pint stock or pig's
pinch thyme	blood
2 or 3 cloves	2–3 tablespoons
pinch marjoram	cream
pinch powdered	
coriander	**to garnish:**
pepper	lemon
3–4 oz. lard or fat	parsley

1 Cut the pork into large dice.
2 Marinate for 24 hours in wine, onions and herbs.
3 Next day drain off marinade into bowl.
4 Melt lard in a heavy saucepan and brown meat over heat.
5 Sprinkle with flour.
6 Add strained marinade liquid and salt to taste, with blood or stock and pepper.
7 Cook for 2¼ hours, stirring frequently.
8 When almost cooked stir in the cream.
9 Garnish with slices of lemon and parsley.

Ragoût of pork

cooking time: 1¾ hours

you will need for 6–8 servings:

sage and onion	½ pint red wine
stuffing, see page 29	¼ pint stock
2 oz. fat, dripping or	¼ teaspoon chilli
lard	powder
2 onions	¼ teaspoon celery salt
2 lb. diced shoulder of	1 bay leaf
pork	salt and pepper
2 sliced green peppers	4 oz. cooked
3 cloves garlic,	macaroni, rice or
chopped	noodles

1 Make stuffing into balls and fry for 2–3 minutes in 1 oz. fat.
2 Melt the rest of the dripping and fry the sliced onions and then the pork until lightly browned.
3 Add all the other ingredients except the macaroni, and cook slowly for 1½ hours.
4 Add the macaroni and the lightly fried stuffing balls just before serving.

Sausages in brine or other liquids

1 Tasty stock is produced if sausages are simmered gently in slightly salted water.
2 Sausages can also be cooked in tomato juice, cider or light ale.

Sausages in stews and casseroles

Few people realise how appetising sausages can be in a stew or casserole. Use either frankfurters or ordinary beef or pork sausages. They lend themselves to both these methods of cooking, but because they cook more quickly, or in the case of frankfurters, need re-heating only, you can reduce the total cooking time.

To Stew Meat

Here are the points to remember:
1 A stew is similar to braised or casseroled meat. It is usually thickened at the end.
2 The secret is to give plenty of time for cooking.
3 It has the great advantage that you can use cheaper cuts of meat and because of this it is an economical as well as an appetising dish.
4 For a quick stew it is helpful to use some of the ready-prepared soups instead of taking the trouble of preparing vegetables; either the canned double thick or packet soups can be used to give a really good sauce for the meat.

Beef goulash

cooking time: 2 hours 45 minutes

you will need for 4 servings:

1–1¼ lb. stewing steak	salt
1 lb. onions	3 large tomatoes
2 oz. dripping or fat	¼ pint water
1 level tablespoon flour	1 lb. potatoes
1–2 tablespoons paprika pepper*	small amount yoghourt

*Paprika pepper is not very hot, but when making a goulash for the first time use rather less than stated, taste, and you can then add extra if liked.

1 Cut steak into neat pieces, slice onions thinly.
2 Fry meat and onions in fat for a few minutes.
3 Stir in flour, paprika pepper, very good pinch salt, skinned chopped tomatoes and water.
4 Bring to boil and cook for a few minutes, stirring well until a smooth liquid.
5 Put on tight fitting lid, cook for about 1½ hours.
6 Slice peeled potatoes and arrange on top.
7 This SHOULD be a very thick stew, but if it looks too dry when potatoes are added, put in an extra tomato and little water.

8 Cook for further 1–1¼ hours.
9 Top with a little yoghourt when serving.

Variations

Using half veal – for Hungarian goulash use half stewing beef and half stewing veal.

With garlic – add 1 or 2 crushed cloves of garlic to meat.

With noodles – omit potatoes and serve with cooked noodles or boiled rice.

For goulash soup – use 2 diced medium potatoes and 1½ pints stock or water. Garnish with tiny dumplings.

Beef stew and noodles

cooking time: 2 hours 15 minutes

you will need for 4 servings:

1 lb. stewing steak	½ pint water
8 oz. onions	1 level teaspoon salt
8 oz. carrots	4 oz. noodles
8 oz. streaky bacon	2 oz. grated cheese
1 oz. fat	

1 Cut steak into 1-inch cubes.
2 Peel onions and chop, peel and slice carrots.
3 Remove the rind from the bacon and cut into small pieces.
4 Melt the fat and fry the meat, onion and bacon for 3–5 minutes.
5 Add the carrots, fry for a further 3–5 minutes.
6 Add the water and bring to the boil, stirring all the time.
7 Reduce the heat and simmer very gently for 1½–2 hours.
8 Half-fill a medium-sized saucepan with water, add salt and bring to the boil. *continued*

9 Add noodles, boil for 10–15 minutes. Strain.

10 Place the noodles on a warmed serving dish, pour the meat stew on top, sprinkle with grated cheese and serve immediately.

Variations

Savoury beef – roll the diced beef in a packet of soup powder – oxtail, tomato, onion flavours are particularly suitable. Serve with the noodles and cheese or creamed potatoes.

Stew with red wine – add crushed clove of garlic to the chopped onions, and use half stock and half cheap red wine.

Beef roulades – have the beef cut into 8 thin slices, and roll each round an uncooked chipolata sausage. Tie or skewer firmly, continue as beef stew.

Paprika beef stew and dumplings – omit bacon and add 2 tomatoes, 2 teaspoons paprika and 1½ pints brown stock. Serve with dumplings.

Chilli hotpot – this is a far less pungent recipe than the true Chilli con carne, see page 63. Use recipe for beef stew and add only 1 teaspoon chilli powder to other seasonings. A crushed clove of garlic can be used.

Mince collops

cooking time: about 1 hour

you will need for 4 servings:

2 onions	2 tomatoes
2 oz. fat	seasoning
1 oz. flour	squeeze lemon juice
½ pint stock or water and stock cube	
1–1¼ lb. minced beef	**to garnish:**
	mixed root vegetables or toast

1 Chop onions finely, fry in hot fat, then add flour and cook gently for a few minutes.

2 Gradually stir in the stock, bring to the boil and cook until smooth sauce.

3 Break minced beef with a fork, add to sauce.

4 Cook gently, stirring from time to time with a wooden spoon to prevent meat forming large lumps at beginning of cooking.

5 Add skinned, chopped tomatoes or tablespoon of purée, seasoning. Cover pan, simmer for 45 minutes.

6 Add little more stock if necessary, but this should be stiff.

7 Stir in lemon juice, put on to hot dish and garnish with vegetables or triangles of toast.

Variations

Curried mince – add good teaspoon curry powder to seasonings.

Tomato mince – use all tomato purée or tomato juice instead of stock.

Creamy mince – use half stock and half milk. Omit tomatoes, use sliced mushrooms instead.

Beef stroganoff 1

cooking time: 15 minutes

you will need for 4 servings:

1 onion	¼ pint and 4 tablespoons
4 oz. butter	
4–8 oz. mushrooms	sour cream or use
1½ lb. lean fillet steak	fresh cream and
seasoning	1–1½ tablespoons lemon juice

1 Fry chopped onion in half the butter, and mushrooms in the remainder.

2 Cut steak into strips, fry in the onion-flavoured butter. Season well.

3 Add warmed cream.

4 Heat together gently.

5 Add mushrooms and serve at once.

Beef stroganoff 2

cooking time: 30 minutes *or* 1 hour 15 minutes

you will need for 4 servings:

1 lb. lean beef	1 pint water or stock,
generous sprinkling salt, pepper, mustard	water to be flavoured with beef extract
pinch curry powder, optional	2 tablespoons tomato juice or purée
1 very large onion	2 tablespoons cream,
3 oz. margarine or butter	preferably sour
1 tablespoon flour	

1 Cut the meat into small pieces or fingers.

2 Sprinkle with salt, pepper, mustard and curry powder.

3 Fry the thinly sliced onion in 2 oz. butter until soft, then work in the flour. Cook gently for a few minutes.

4 Gradually stir in the stock, bring to the boil and allow to thicken.

5 Heat the 1 oz. butter, fry the meat until golden brown.

6 Add to sauce with other ingredients and simmer gently.

7 If using fillet steak cook for 15–20 minutes, but stewing steak could be used and will take about 1 hour to become tender.

8 Serve on hot rice.

Variation

With brandy – for very special occasions add a little brandy before serving.

Chinese beef

cooking time: 20 minutes

you will need for 4 servings:

1 clove garlic	1 beef stock cube
1 small red pepper	2 level tablespoons
8 sliced water	cornflour
chestnuts*	1 pint hot water
1 small can bean	2 tablespoons soy
sprouts, drained*	sauce*
2 oz. mushrooms,	2 tablespoons red
sliced	wine
2 tablespoons oil	12 oz. diced beef
	6 oz. noodles

*Obtainable from grocers selling Chinese products.

1 Chop the garlic very finely and chop the red pepper, taking care to remove all seeds.

2 Lightly fry the vegetables in the oil for about 5 minutes.

3 Crumble in the beef cube, add the cornflour and stir in well.

4 Add the hot water and stir till boiling.

5 Add the soy sauce, wine and cooked beef and simmer gently for about 10 minutes.

6 Serve hot with cooked noodles, see page 65.

Lamb and rice hotpot

cooking time: 1¼ hours

you will need for 4 servings:

2 onions	good pinch salt
2 carrots	meat stock or water
1 turnip	8 best end neck lamb
bouquet garni (parsley,	chops
thyme, bay leaf)	4 oz. rice
few peppercorns	lemon slices to
	garnish

1 Slice vegetables thickly and put them into a large saucepan with *bouquet garni*, peppercorns and salt.

2 Add sufficient stock or water to nearly cover them. Place chops on top.

3 Cover with tightly fitting lid, bring to boil.

4 Simmer gently until meat is tender, approximately 1 hour.

5 If necessary, add more stock from time to time to replace that which has boiled away.

6 Arrange meat and vegetables in dish and keep warm in slow oven (300°F. – Gas Mark 2).

7 Strain meat stock. Use to boil the rice in.

8 When cooked, strain and place on large dish with meat arranged on top.

9 Garnish with sliced lemon.

Variations

Creole lamb – add crushed clove garlic to onions, together with good pinch curry or chilli powder. Omit carrots and use sliced green pepper instead.

Courgette lamb – omit carrots and use 3 skinned sliced tomatoes instead. 15 minutes before the end of the cooking time, add about 1–2 lb. (depending on other vegetables being served) of tiny well-washed courgettes.

Spicy lamb stew – add 3 oz. diced bacon, grated rind of a lemon, little chopped celery, crushed clove of garlic and very good pinch cayenne pepper to ingredients.

Lamb with rice – cook as the recipe for 45 minutes, add rice, 4 skinned, sliced tomatoes and 1 oz. raisins with another ½ pint water, if it seems dry. Cook gently for 20 minutes, or until rice is soft.

Beef and vegetable crumble

cooking time: 30 minutes

you will need for 4 servings:

large can of beef	1½ oz. butter or
and vegetables	margarine
4 oz. flour	1 oz. finely grated
pinch salt	cheese

1 Put the meat into an ovenproof dish.

2 Sieve flour and salt, rub in butter or margarine and add cheese. Press over top of meat and bake in a moderate oven (357°F. – Gas Mark 4–5) for approximately 30 minutes.

Haricot lamb

cooking time: 1½–1¾ hours

you will need for 4 servings:

6 oz. haricot beans
2 onions
2 carrots
2 oz. mushrooms
1½ lb. lamb, middle
   neck, scrag or
   breast
1 oz. flour
seasoning
1 oz. butter
1 pint stock or water
   and stock cube
little chopped parsley

1 Soak the beans overnight in water.
2 Peel and slice the vegetables finely.
3 Cut the meat in serving pieces.
4 Toss in well seasoned flour.
5 Melt the butter in a saucepan and brown the meat.
6 Add the onions, carrots and mushrooms and colour gently.
7 Drain the haricot beans and add to the stew.
8 Pour in the stock.
9 Cover and simmer gently for 1½–1¾ hours.
10 Turn on to hot dish and sprinkle with chopped parsley.

Variation

Haricot mutton – use mutton instead of lamb, and allow about 2–2¼ hours' cooking time.

Savoury minced steak with soufflé topping

cooking time: 30–35 minutes

you will need for 4 servings:

1 small green pepper
1 small onion
2 oz. mushrooms
2 tomatoes
1 tablespoon oil
16 oz. can minced
   steak
pinch mixed herbs or
   oregano
seasoning

for topping:
2 oz. Cheddar cheese,
   finely grated
3 tablespoons
   evaporated milk
2 eggs, separated
salt, cayenne pepper

for garnish:
parsley

1 Remove seeds from pepper, peel onion, mushrooms and tomatoes. Chop vegetables and fry in heated oil from 2–3 minutes, then add herbs and seasoning.
2 Place the minced steak in an ovenproof dish and top with the vegetables.
3 Make the soufflé topping by melting the cheese in the evaporated milk in a basin placed over a saucepan of hot water. Allow to cool slightly, then stir in egg yolks and seasoning. Whisk the egg whites until stiff and fold into cheese mixture. Place on top of the vegetables.
4 Bake in a pre-heated moderate oven (375°F. – Gas Mark 4) for 20–25 minutes. Serve at once, garnished with parsley.

Irish stew

cooking time: about 2¼ hours

you will need for 4 servings:

1–1½ lb. scrag end of
   neck of lamb
1 lb. potatoes
8—12 oz. onions
¾ pint water
salt and pepper

to garnish:
peas
carrots

1 Wash the meat and cut into neat pieces.
2 If using new potatoes, cut one or two in halves, or if using old potatoes, cut one large one into small slices.
3 Slice the onions.
4 Put the meat, pieces of potato, and the sliced onions in a pan, adding about ¾ pint water and salt and pepper.
5 Bring slowly to the boil, remove any scum, lower the heat and simmer gently for just over 1½ hours.
6 Add remaining potatoes with a little more salt, and continue cooking for about 40 minutes.
7 Pile the meat and stock in the centre of a hot dish with the potatoes round and garnish with freshly cooked peas and carrots.

Mutton and cabbage

cooking time: 2½ hours

you will need for 4 servings:

1½ lb. mutton
1½ lb. cabbage
1½ teaspoons salt
1 pint boiling water
8 black peppercorns
small Savoy cabbage
1 tablespoon chopped
   parsley

1 Wash meat and cut in pieces.
2 Parboil the cabbage and slice.
3 Arrange meat and cabbage in layers, placing the fat pieces of meat in bottom of saucepan.
4 Sprinkle with salt, add water.
5 Tie peppercorns in small piece of muslin. Boil with meat.

6 Let simmer under tightly fitting lid for 2 hours. Remove peppercorns.

7 Add Savoy cabbage cut in slices and cook 30 minutes more.

8 Sprinkle with parsley and serve.

9 Gourmets prefer this dish when warmed up three times.

10 Remember to use piping hot plates for serving.

Creamy veal stew

cooking time: 1½ hours

you will need for 4 servings:

1½ lb. stewing veal	**for the sauce:**
1 onion	½ oz. butter
2 cloves	½ oz. flour
1 carrot, sliced	¼ pint milk
salt and pepper	4 small onions
1 pint water	
1 lb. chopped potatoes	

1 Cut veal into pieces.

2 Insert cloves in the onion.

3 Put meat, onion, carrot, seasoning, and water into a pan.

4 Simmer for 1 hour, adding potatoes for last 30 minutes.

5 Make white sauce with butter, flour, milk and ¼ pint of the veal stock.

6 Put in the onions and simmer for 30 minutes, adding a little extra stock if needed.

7 Add veal and potatoes only to the sauce and heat through.

Sour sweet veal

cooking time: about 30 minutes

you will need for 4 servings:

4 veal chops OR 1 lb. fillet of veal, cut into neat pieces	1 lb. sliced onions
1 oz. flour	4 oz. cooked lima beans*
2 teaspoons salt	¼ pint and 4 tablespoons peach juice
¼ teaspoon pepper	
2 oz. fat	4 halved peaches, canned are better in this recipe
1 clove garlic	

*If not available use haricot beans.

1 Toss chops or meat in a mixture of flour, salt and pepper.

2 Brown in hot fat, with the split garlic, in a heavy frying pan.

3 Remove garlic. Add the onions, beans and peach juice to the meat together with extra salt, if required.

4 Bring to the boil, lower the heat and simmer for about 30 minutes, adding the sliced peaches for the last 10 minutes.

5 Transfer to serving dish. This is delicious with cooked rice.

Variation

Spicy sour-sweet veal – to accentuate the mixture of sour and sweet in this dish, add a few drops of soy sauce and vinegar or lemon juice as well.

To Boil Meat

The terms 'boiled gammon', 'boiled beef', are always used. In practice, as so often happens in cooking, you allow the liquid to **simmer** only. If you boil the meat it is likely to be toughened and spoilt.

Here are the points to remember:

1 The water should cover the meat.

2 Longer cooking time should be allowed for cheaper cuts of meat.

3 Time the meat as given in each recipe and then test to see if it is tender.

4 If it is quite tender a little while before needed for serving you can take the pan off the heat, leave the meat in the hot liquid, and reheat at the last minute.

5 If, by chance, you find that the meat is not as tender as you would wish, you can then give a little longer simmering.

6 Remember that times will vary a little, according to the amount of room in the pan. If you have a piece of meat fitting tightly in the saucepan, it is inclined to take longer to cook than if the water can move slowly, but freely, around it.

7 Salted meat always needs a little longer cooking than fresh.

To boil beef

Boiled brisket of beef (1)

Brisket of beef (2) gives lightly cooked vegetables, which look more pleasant with the dish. But if you wish the vegetables to flavour the meat, put them in at the beginning of the cooking time.

To serve, lift the beef on to a dish and strain the liquid into a sauce boat to serve with it.

Instead of calculating the cooking time by the method in the following recipe, you may prefer to allow 35–40 minutes per lb. steady simmering and 35–40 minutes over; or use 45–50 minutes per lb. with the water hardly moving and 45–50 minutes over.

Boiled brisket of beef (2)

cooking time: 2 hours, salted; 1½ hours unsalted

you will need for 6 servings:

2 lb. brisket of beef, salted or unsalted	little butter
	1 medium-sized onion
water to cover	1 oz. flour
1 large onion	
4–5 cloves	**to garnish:**
2 carrots	1 large apple
1 bay leaf	butter for frying
sprig of parsley	

1 If your joint of beef is salted soak for several hours in cold water, place in fresh cold water, bring to the boil gently and allow to simmer for 1 hour, then change the water.
2 If beef is unsalted simply cover the meat with cold water.
3 Add the peeled large onion, studded with cloves, the quartered carrots, bay leaf and parsley to the meat.
4 Bring to the boil and cook gently, allowing 20 minutes per lb. and 20 minutes over.
5 Meanwhile heat the butter in a small pan, add the chopped medium-sized onion and cook until golden brown.
6 Sprinkle in the flour, stir well, and cook for a few moments.
7 Gradually add ½ pint boiling stock from the beef, stirring all the time.
8 Cook gently for 20 minutes, stirring frequently.
9 When cooked, slice the meat, cover with the onion sauce, and garnish with slices of apple fried in butter.

Stuffed brisket of beef – after soaking the beef, dry well, split through centre to form a 'pocket', put in stuffing, taking care not to over salt. Tie the joint firmly and cook as before.

Pressed brisket of beef – cook salt brisket of beef as before.

Lift out of the liquid and put the beef into a saucepan or a tin, see Boiled tongue, page 92. Dissolve 1 teaspoon powdered gelatine in ¼ pint of the hot stock. Pour over the beef, cover, and put with a weight on top for some hours until cold and the jelly is set.

Boiled silverside – this is cooked in exactly the same way as the brisket. It is generally a more expensive joint to buy.

When ordering salt silverside or brisket, remember it has to be in brine for several days to be at its best and you should therefore give the butcher ample notice.

Wet pickle for silverside or brisket

cooking time: 5 minutes

you will need:

1 lb. kitchen salt	1 gallon water
6 oz. moist brown sugar	silverside or brisket
½ oz. saltpetre	

1 Put the salt, sugar, saltpetre and water into a large pan, bring to the boil and boil for 5 minutes.
2 Skim well and strain into a large basin or pickling jar and leave until quite cold.
3 Remove any discoloured parts from the meat and wipe thoroughly with a damp cloth.
4 Put into the cold pickle, cover and keep in a cool larder for 10–14 days. Turn the meat every day.
5 Allow to soak overnight in cold water before cooking.

To boil lamb

Boiled lamb or mutton and caper sauce

cooking time: 1½ hours for lamb
2 hours for mutton

you will need for 4 servings:

1–1½ lb. scrag or middle neck of lamb or mutton	water
	seasoning
	caper sauce, see
carrots	below
onions	

1 Put the meat into the pan with the vegetables, cover with cold water, bring to the boil, skim.
2 Add seasoning, lower the heat and simmer gently for approximately 1½–2 hours.
3 Lift meat and vegetables on to a hot dish and make the caper sauce, using half milk and half the mutton or lamb stock. Serve with lamb.
4 Extra stock can be served separately.
5 This dish looks more colourful and interesting if a few carrots and onions are cooked separately and served on top of those cooked with the meat.
6 Any stock or vegetables remaining make a good basis for a soup.

Caper sauce

Use the basic recipe for White sauce, page 86, but instead of ½ pint milk, use a good ¼ pint milk and a good ¼ pint of stock, so giving a slightly thinner coating of sauce.

When the sauce is thickened, stir in 2–3 teaspoons of capers and a few drops of vinegar from the bottle.

Boiled leg of lamb or mutton

For a large family, or a more elegant and lean joint, a leg or half a leg of lamb or mutton can be served instead of scrag or middle neck. For lamb, allow a good 20 minutes per lb. and 20 minutes over; for mutton 25–30 minutes per lb. and 25–30 minutes over.

To boil veal

Veal is not really a suitable joint for boiling unless you wish to cook it this way before putting it into a fricassée. In this case put the veal into a pan with cold water, a pinch of mixed herbs, and 1–2 pieces of lemon peel. Simmer gently, allowing 25–30 minutes per lb., and 25–30 minutes over. When making the fricassée, use half stock and half water.

Breast of veal – stuffed, boned and rolled. Use stuffing as page 28. Add to water 1 bay leaf, salt and pepper, sliced carrots, leeks and onions.

To boil pork

Boiled belly of pork

Belly of pork, which is rather fat by itself, is excellent to boil and serve cold with other cold meats.

Put into a pan, adding cold water to cover and onions to taste if wished, although these can be omitted. Bring to the boil and skim the surface. Lower the heat, and simmer gently, allowing about 40 minutes per lb. and 40 minutes over.

Pickled pork

cooking time: 2 hours 15 minutes

you will need:

1–1½ lb. breast or thin flank pork	**for marinade pickle:**
	½ pint wine or cider vinegar
salt	4 tablespoons oil
water, to cover	12 peppercorns
carrots	pinch thyme
1 onion	2–3 spring onions or handful chives
	2 onions

1 Place the pork on a layer of salt, then cover it with more salt.
2 Allow it to stand for 24 hours. Rub off salt. Place in a saucepan and cover with cold water.
3 Simmer the meat very slowly, for 2 hours, adding the onion and a few carrots.
4 When cooked, allow the meat to cool in its liquor.
5 Slice it when cold. Then make the pickle mixture as follows.
6 Place the vinegar, oil, peppercorns, thyme, chopped chives or spring onions and sliced onions in a saucepan. Bring to the boil.
7 Allow to boil quickly for 15 minutes, then let the marinade cool.
8 Pour it over the sliced pork and allow to stand for 3–4 hours, turn slices from time to time.

To boil bacon or ham

cooking time: as table, page 11

you will need:
piece of bacon or ham
water

1 Unless the piece of bacon or ham is very mild, soak it for several hours or overnight in cold water.
2 Throw away this water.
3 Put into a pan and completely cover with cold water. Bring steadily to the boil, skim if necessary.
4 Lower the heat and simmer very gently indeed.
5 Prime ham or bacon will take approximately 20–25 minutes per lb., and 20–25 minutes over; the cheaper cuts, see page 11, need up to 45 minutes per lb. and 45 minutes over.

6 It is advisable to allow the bacon to stand, if possible, in the water when it has been cooked if you intend to serve it cold, for if it cools in the liquid it does keep very much more moist.
7 Lift out, strip off the skin, and sprinkle the fat with crisp crumbs.

Boiled bacon in ale or cider

Cook in exactly the same way as in the preceding recipe, but use either light ale or cider. Flavour this with 1–2 bay leaves, 2–3 cloves, and just a little brown sugar.

Glazed boiled bacon – when a piece of bacon or ham has been boiled, it can be glazed in the oven, and you will find details of this under Baking, see page 36.

Sweet boiled bacon – if preferred, the bacon or ham can be given a sweet flavour by cooking either in canned pineapple juice or water with a little lemon or orange juice.

To Fricassée Meat

For a fricassée, milk and perhaps a little cream, is used with stock to make a creamy white sauce to which cooked meat is added. This is an ideal way of serving meat when you wish a really creamy consistency and is particularly suitable for young lamb and veal. Care must be taken when cooking the sauce that the mixture does not boil, otherwise it will stick and burn, and if lemon juice has been added it will curdle.

A rather more elaborate version of a fricassée is called a blanquette and a recipe for a blanquette of veal is given which could be used also for young lamb.

Fricassée of meat

cooking time: 15–20 minutes

you will need for 4 servings:
1–1½ lb. cooked meat
white sauce made
with:
1 oz. flour
1 oz. fat
¼ pint meat stock

nearly ½ pint milk with
a little cream
seasoning
squeeze lemon juice

1 Make the sauce, and add the neatly sliced or diced meat.

2 Season very well, and when the lemon juice has been added, be careful not to boil.
3 This is suitable for lamb and for veal. Any lean pork can be served in a fricassée, although most people find it rather rich.
4 For a more elaborate dish you can use equal quantities of stock, milk and white wine.
5 Serve in a border of creamed potatoes or cooked rice.

Blanquette of veal (1)

cooking time: 1 nour 35 minutes

you will need for 4 servings:
1 lb. veal, diced
2 onions
bouquet garni
1 pint white stock OR
water and chicken
bouillon cube
2 oz. butter
2 oz. flour

¼ pint cream or
evaporated milk
1 or 2 egg yolks
1 tablespoon lemon
juice

to garnish:
bacon rolls
parsley

1 Put veal, onions and herbs into pan with stock.
2 Simmer gently until tender.

3 Strain, keep the meat hot.

4 Make a sauce with the butter, flour and 1 pint stock, cook for 2 minutes.

5 Add the evaporated milk and reheat.

6 Stir in the egg yolk and lemon juice, reheat, but do not boil.

7 Pour over the veal and garnish with bacon rolls and chopped parsley.

Variation

Blanquette of veal (2) – add 3 rashers diced streaky bacon to veal. Add strips of canned red pepper to sauce as a garnish.

To Curry Meat

A curry is not only an excellent way of using left-over meat, but of serving fresh meats of various kinds in a spicy sauce. You may like to vary the recipes by adding less or more curry powder or other spices.

Where a recipe says curry paste this can be substituted, but many people feel the best blending of flavours is given by using half curry powder and half curry paste, or by making up your own 'blend' of curry powder by using ginger, spice, turmeric, coriander and any other spices that particularly appeal.

All curries should be served with plain boiled or saffron rice.

To cook curry

Because the curry sauce is a fairly thick one, care must be taken that the liquid does not evaporate too quickly and stick, so cover the pan firmly. Both oven and saucepan methods of cooking are perfectly satisfactory.

To curry cooked meat

One of the most popular ways of serving a curry is to use up the remains of cooked meat. The secret is to make the curry sauce, see recipe opposite, and to allow it to simmer for some little time, add the meat and cook very gently so that it does not come stringy with over-cooking. It will need approximately ¾–1 hour slow cooking, so that it absorbs the flavour. This is the basic curry, but here are suggestions for giving variations of flavour.

Beef

As this has a fairly strong flavour, increase the amount of curry paste slightly and add a little horseradish or horseradish sauce.

Lamb or mutton

This is improved by a slightly sweeter taste, so add 2–3 teaspoons of ham or extra chutney.

Veal

As this has a delicate flavour, it is very pleasant if the cream is added.

Pork

Use the lean part only and use a rather larger cooking apple than usual to give a sharper taste.

Curry sauce

cooking time: a good hour

you will need:

1 medium-sized onion	1 dessertspoon chutney
1 cooking apple	
1 oz. butter	1 tablespoon desiccated coconut
1 level tablespoon curry powder	
	1 dessertspoon sultanas
1 teaspoon curry paste	
	1 teaspoon lemon juice
1 level tablespoon cornflour	
	salt
½ pint stock or water	1–2 tablespoons milk or cream*

*This can be omitted with meat curries, except with creamed veal curry.

1 Chop the onion and cooking apple and fry lightly in the butter.

2 Add the curry powder, paste and cornflour. Stir until blended.

3 Cook a few minutes, then stir in the stock or water.

4 Bring to the boil, stirring all the time.

5 Add the chutney, coconut and sultanas.

6 Cover and simmer for at least an hour.

7 Stir in the lemon juice, seasoning and the milk or cream if used.

Curried meat balls

cooking time: 45 minutes–1 hour

you will need for 4 servings:

for the meat balls:	1 beaten egg yolk
1 lb. minced chuck	curry sauce, see
steak	page 73
1 small chopped onion	
2 tablespoons	**to garnish:**
chopped parsley	lemon slices
1 oz. margarine	parsley sprigs
1 oz. white	
breadcrumbs	**to serve:**
1 teaspoon lemon	boiled rice
juice	
1 teaspoon salt	
pinch pepper	

1 Mix together all the meat ball ingredients and shape into twelve balls.
2 Make curry sauce, then drop in the meat balls.
3 Cover and cook gently for 45 minutes to 1 hour.
4 Garnish with lemon slices and parsley sprigs.
5 Serve with boiled rice.

To curry uncooked meats

Naturally uncooked meat must be cooked well but make the curry sauce and allow this to cook for about 30 minutes, or even longer if wished before putting in the meat. Add the diced meat and simmer very gently for about 2 hours, although time varies according to toughness of the meat used. You may need to add little extra liquid to the sauce, but this should not be necessary with a tightly fitting lid.

Beef curry – increase amount of onion and seasoning.

Mutton curry – make the sauce sweeter, you can add one or two chopped tomatoes, soaked dried beans or peas.

Veal curry – add diced green pepper, extra lemon juice, paprika or cayenne pepper.

Pork curry – increase amount of dried fruit and apple.

Accompaniments to curry

Chutney – a chutney of some kind is generally served. Mango or apple are good.

Chapatis, parathas, poppadums – Indian breads which can be bought from shops selling a good variety of imported foods.
Poppadums should be fried for a few seconds.

Bombay duck – strong-smelling dried fish. Fry in a little fat. Crumble over the curry.

Sliced peppers – both red and green can be used with sliced onion and lemon juice.

Chopped chillis – use sparingly as they are very hot.

Chopped fresh herbs – mix with a little sugar.

Pickles – gherkins, sliced or whole; pickled red cabbage or pickled onions.

Fruit and nuts – sliced banana or apple, sliced lemon, shredded or desiccated coconut, fresh or salted peanuts.

To Steam Meat

Meat to be steamed should be put between two plates with a little seasoning, butter or other fat if allowed, or a little milk, and cooked over a pan of boiling water until tender. This is considered an easily digested form of cooking, but if being given to people on a fat-free diet, you must cut off every particle of fat and season only before steaming. You may prefer to wrap the meat in foil and put it in a steamer over boiling water.

To Use Left-over Cooked Meats

Great care must be taken that cooked meat has been stored in a really cold place so there is no fear of it being spoiled, and as far as possible, when it is first cooked, cook for the minimum time.

When using the cooked meat in a made-up dish, reheat this for the minimum time so you do not lose the flavour of the meat.

The following recipes give ideas for using meat that is already cooked, but as well as these you can:

1 Reheat in good sauce – make sauce first, then heat the meat for few minutes only.
2 Use as filling for pancakes. Mince the meat and mix with
  (a) brown or espagnole sauce, see page 84.
  (b) cheese, white or onion sauce, see pages 85–86.
  (c) tomato sauce, see page 85, or tomato purée,
3 Make into a mould, see page 82, but since cooked meat will be dryer, add little extra liquid in recipes.

Beef rolls

cooking time: 25 minutes

you will need for 4 servings:

2 eggs	2 tablespoons cream
1 tablespoon milk	2 eating apples
knob butter	salt and pepper
4 tablespoons sultanas	4 large slices cold roast beef
4 tablespoons creamed potatoes	½ pint white stock

1 Scramble the eggs with the milk and butter.
2 Mix with the sultanas, potatoes and cream.
3 Dice the apple finely and add to the mixture.
4 Season carefully and put a spoonful of the mixture on each slice of meat.
5 Roll up the meat and put into an ovenproof dish.
6 Pour in the stock and bake in a very moderate oven (350°F. – Gas Mark 3) for 20 minutes.
7 Baste the meat with the juice during cooking.

Durham cutlets

cooking time: about 20 minutes

you will need for 4 servings:

8–12 oz. cooked meat	4 oz. breadcrumbs
1 oz. margarine	1 egg
small chopped onion	2 tablespoons crisp breadcrumbs for coating
1 oz. flour	
¼ pint gravy, or stock, or water flavoured with beef or yeast extract	2 oz. dripping or lard
salt and pepper	**to garnish:**
pinch mixed herbs	fried tomatoes
1 tablespoon chopped parsley	parsley

1 Mince or chop the meat.
2 Heat margarine in a saucepan and fry the onion.
3 Stir in flour, cook for a few minutes, then gradually stir in liquid.
4 Bring to the boil and cook until a thick sauce.
5 Add seasoning, herbs, parsley, meat and breadcrumbs.
6 Let the mixture cool, form into four cutlet shapes and coat with beaten egg and crumbs.
7 Fry steadily in hot fat for 4 minutes each side, then lower heat and cook for further 4 minutes to ensure they are heated right through.
8 Drain on crumpled tissue paper and garnish with fried tomatoes and parsley.

Variations

Herby cutlets – add 1 good tablespoon chopped fresh herbs as well as parsley.
Tomato cutlets – use tomato juice instead of gravy.

Rissoles

These are basically the same recipe as Durham cutlets above. Instead of forming into a cutlet shape, the mixture is made into a round cake and coated, then fried.

Variations

Omit breadcrumbs – put in a little more mashed potato.

For a creamy texture – use milk instead of stock.

For a more spicy flavour – use a little curry powder or Worcestershire sauce.

Use tomato purée – or juice instead of stock.

Beef rissoles – add 1 extra chopped onion.

Lamb rissoles – add 1 teaspoon each thyme, sage and marjoram.

Potato pie

cooking time: 45–50 minutes

you will need for 4 servings:

1 lb. potatoes	salt and pepper
¼ pint good stock	1 small onion
½–1 lb. cooked minced beef	1 oz. butter
2 chopped tomatoes	little egg for brushing

1 Peel and slice the potatoes and cook in boiling salted water until tender.
2 Drain and mash.
3 Add stock to the meat with tomatoes and seasoning.
4 Chop the onion and cook gently in butter and mix into the meat.
5 Turn into a casserole and top with the potato.
6 Brush with a little beaten egg and cook in a moderate oven (375°F. – Gas Mark 4) for 20 minutes.

Shepherd's pie – this is another name for potato pie, although some people like to serve sliced potatoes instead of mashed potatoes on top of the mixture.

Cross-over patties

cooking time: 15–20 minutes

you will need for 9 patties:

8 oz. short crust pastry	1 level teaspoon made-mustard
6 oz. corned beef or cold cooked lamb, beef or veal, minced	1 large egg, beaten egg or milk to glaze parsley to garnish
1½ oz. fresh white breadcrumbs	

1 Make pastry and cut into nine 3½-inch squares.
2 Mix well together the meat, crumbs and mustard then bind with the egg.
3 Divide into nine equal portions and form each into a sausage shape. Place these diagonally across the squares of pastry. Moisten opposite corners of each with water, then fold one over the other, partially enclosing the meat. Brush tops with beaten egg or milk then transfer patties to a greased baking tray.
4 Bake towards the top of a hot oven (425–450°F. – Gas Mark 6–7) for 15–20 minutes. Garnish with parsley.

Savoury platter

cooking time: 20 minutes

you will need for 4 servings:

1 small onion	salt and pepper
1 oz. dripping	4 hard-boiled eggs
1 oz. plain flour	½ pint cheese sauce, see page 85
12 oz. cooked minced beef	2 level tablespoons browned breadcrumbs
½ pint water	
¼ teaspoon meat extract	

1 Chop the onion and cook in dripping until tender.
2 Stir in the flour and meat, add the water, meat extract and seasoning to taste.
3 Simmer gently for 15 minutes, turn into a wide dish.
4 Halve the eggs and place flat side down on top of the meat, pour over the sauce.
5 Sprinkle with crumbs and brown the surface under a hot grill.

Welsh beef pie

cooking time: 30 minutes

you will need for 4 servings:

1½ lb. leeks	1 small can tomato soup or ½ pint tomato sauce, see page 85
4 oz. fat bacon	
12 oz. minced cooked beef	
salt and pepper	stock or gravy
horseradish sauce	2 oz. browned breadcrumbs
	2 oz. grated cheese

1 Prepare the leeks. Cut them into short lengths and boil until tender.
2 Drain very well.
3 Cut bacon into pieces and fry lightly.
4 Season the meat well with salt, pepper and horseradish sauce.
5 Put alternate layers of bacon, leeks and meat into a greased 2 pint casserole.
6 Measure the soup or sauce and make up to ¾ pint with stock or gravy.

7 Pour over the ingredients in the dish.

8 Mix the breadcrumbs and cheese together and sprinkle over the top.

9 Bake for 25–30 minutes in hot oven (425–450°F. – Gas Mark 6–7).

Lamb pies

cooking time: 45 minutes

you will need for 4 servings:

¾–1 lb. cold lamb	3 peppercorns
3 oz. boiled bacon or ham	4 tablespoons stock
1½ oz. butter	1 teaspoon flour
1 shallot or onion	12 oz. short or flaky pastry
6 large mushrooms	1 egg yolk
3 cloves	

1 Remove any skin and gristle from the lamb, chop it and the bacon or ham fairly finely.

2 Melt 1 oz. of the butter and cook the chopped shallot and mushrooms in it until soft.

3 Simmer the cloves and peppercorns in the stock for 15 minutes.

4 Make a sauce with the rest of the butter, flour and the strained stock.

5 Stir in the meat and mushroom mixture and allow to cool.

6 Line deep patty cases with the pastry.

7 Fill with the mixture, cover with more pastry, and decorate with pastry leaves.

8 Brush with beaten egg yolk and bake for 20 minutes in a hot oven (450°F. – Gas Mark 7).

Fried vealets

cooking time: 5 minutes

you will need for 4 servings:

1–1¼ lb. cooked veal	breadcrumbs
salt and pepper	oil for frying
1 oz. flour	mixed vegetables
2 egg whites*	
*Or 1 whole egg	

1 Cut the cooked veal into walnut-sized pieces.

2 Season them with salt and pepper.

3 Coat them with flour, beaten egg white or whole egg, then breadcrumbs.

4 Heat the oil until it gives off a faint blue smoke.

5 Plunge in the crumbed veal.

6 Allow to cook until golden brown.

7 Drain well before serving with a medley of separately cooked vegetables.

Veal and ham rolls

cooking time: 10–12 minutes

you will need for 4 servings:

1 teaspoon thyme	1 egg
1 tablespoon chopped parsley	8 thin slices ham
2 oz. fresh breadcrumbs	8 thin slices cooked veal
juice 1 lemon	crisp breadcrumbs
1 oz. suet	fat for frying

1 Mix thyme and parsley with breadcrumbs.

2 Bind the mixture together with lemon juice, suet and a little beaten egg.

3 Spread the mixture quite thinly on each slice of ham.

4 Lay a slice of veal on top.

5 Trim and roll each sandwich tightly.

6 Either tie or skewer.

7 Dip in egg and breadcrumbs and fry in shallow fat.

Bacon and cider cobbler

cooking time: 25–30 minutes

you will need for 4 servings:

4 slices cooked bacon, ½ inch thick	1 teaspoon sage
½ pint cider or ale	salt and pepper
2 oz. margarine	1 egg
6 oz. flour, with plain flour use 1 teaspoon baking powder	milk

1 Place the bacon in a fireproof dish and add the cider or ale.

2 Put into hot oven (425–450°F. – Gas Mark 6–7), while making up dough by rubbing the margarine into the flour.

3 Add the sage, salt and pepper and mix to soft dough with the egg and a little milk.

4 Roll out and cut into four pieces the size of the bacon slices.

5 Take the dish from the oven and lay the dough slices on top of the bacon.

6 Brush over with a little milk and bake for further 15 minutes at the same temperature, or until the top is crisp and the underneath of the dough has absorbed the liquid and adheres to the bacon.

Meat croquettes

cooking time: 15–20 minutes

you will need for 4 servings:

12 oz. cooked meat	2 teaspoons chopped
1 oz. butter or	gherkins
margarine	3 oz. soft fresh
1 oz. flour	breadcrumbs
¼ pint milk	seasoning
2 teaspoons chopped	
parsley	

to coat:
1 egg, 2 oz. breadcrumbs

1 Mince the meat or chop very finely.
2 Make a thick sauce of the butter or margarine, flour and milk, add the parsley, gherkins and the meat. Blend well, then stir in breadcrumbs and seasoning. Allow to cool and form into about 8 finger shapes.
3 Brush with beaten egg and coat in crisp breadcrumbs.
4 Fry in hot fat until crisp and brown. Drain well on absorbent paper. Serve hot or cold.

Variations

Beef – add a little grated horseradish or horseradish cream to mixture, or season well with mustard.

Lamb or mutton – use chopped mint in addition to parsley, or use instead of parsley. Add 2 teaspoons capers.

Pork – add chopped fresh or dried sage to flavour, together with finely chopped shallot or chives.

Veal – blend 1–2 teaspoons paprika with sauce.

Meat Salads

Most meats are really good served with a salad. Remember the following, however:
1 Sliced meat dries very quickly so do not leave it exposed to the air for any length of time. If you do the meat dries, curls and looks extremely unappetising, apart from being a potential source of danger, in that it begins to spoil in a warm place.
2 Be adventurous with meat salads. Add a little fruit to the salads.
For example:

Beef
(a) **Pickled red cabbage,** together with diced sharp apples, make a good accompaniment to beef.
(b) **A little horseradish cream** or grated horseradish can be added to mayonnaise for extra flavour.
(c) **Rings of pineapple** give a fresh bite in a beef salad.

Lamb or mutton
(a) **All berry fruits,** grapes and diced apples are excellent in a lamb salad.
(b) Blend a little **mint sauce** with French dressing or mayonnaise to serve with cold lamb.
(c) **All fruit jellies,** as well as redcurrant jelly, can be served with cold lamb or mutton.

Veal
(a) Cold veal can be delicious. It is inclined to lack flavour, so use plenty of **diced onion,** cucumber and gherkins in the salad.
(b) Rather **mild flavoured fruits,** such as apricots, fresh or canned, can be served with the salad.
(c) Cold veal can be a little dry and lacking in fat, so a **rich mayonnaise** is an ideal accompaniment.

Pork
(a) Since cold pork is a fairly rich meat for a salad, make a good contrast by adding **prunes, apples or pineapples,** or other sharp fruit.
(b) A very rich mayonnaise is not a good accompaniment to a pork salad. Toss the salad instead either in **lemon juice** or a rather sharp vinegar dressing.

Bacon and ham
(a) Cooked bacon or ham are two of the best meats to serve with salad and your salad can contain endless variety.
(b) **Pineapple** gives it a pleasing bite.
(c) **Cooked or canned prunes** give richness.
(d) **Apples, oranges,** or any rather sharp fruit are excellent.
(e) Because bacon and ham are fairly rich in

texture, a rather **sweet mayonnaise** or French dressing is delicious with the salad.

(f) Roll ham or bacon to a horn shape and fill with **cream cheese** or sweetcorn.

Canned meats

(a) Take extra care when preparing a salad to serve with canned meats.

(b) If your salad contains lots of gay, interesting ingredients, you will find that the canned meat no longer looks like a 'made-in-a-hurry' meal.

Sausages

(a) Serve a really **spicy dressing** with cold sausages and salad.

(b) Add a little **horseradish sauce,** chilli sauce or Worcestershire sauce to mayonnaise, or blend plenty of made mustard with the mayonnaise.

(c) **Fruit** such as apples, segments of orange or grapefruit, blend well with sausages.

(d) **Grated cheese** topped with chipolata sausages on a green salad is very tasty.

Pretty chic salad

no cooking

you will need for 4 servings:

2 heads chicory	parsley
3 sticks celery	4 oz. sliced cooked
1 dessert apple	ham
salad cream or	4 oz. tongue
mayonnaise	lettuce, watercress or
	shredded cabbage

1 Clean the chicory and celery and cut into large squares.

2 Wipe and core apple without peeling it and then dice.

3 Turn these into the salad cream, mix well and heap on to a plate, sprinkling with finely chopped parsley.

4 Dice the meats and place round the salad.

5 Surround the whole with the lettuce, watercress or cabbage and chill.

Variation

With walnut – add walnut halves and an extra apple, and reduce amount of meat.

Bacon salad

no cooking

you will need for 4 servings:

8–12oz. cooked bacon	dash Tabasco sauce
8 oz. cooked new	dash lemon juice
potatoes	salt and pepper
chopped mint	shredded lettuce
chopped parsley	radishes
4 tablespoons	cucumber
mayonnaise	
1 tablespoon tomato	
sauce	

1 Dice bacon and potatoes and toss with the mint and parsley.

2 Blend together in a basin the mayonnaise, sauces and lemon juice and season well.

3 Add the bacon mixture and fold in carefully.

4 Pile this mixture on to shredded lettuce.

5 Garnish with radishes and cucumber.

Oriental pork and rice salad

cooking time: 15 minutes

you will need for 4 servings:

6 oz. long-grained	1 tablespoon currants
Patna rice	1 large tomato,
cut clove garlic,	skinned, seeded and
optional	chopped
3 tablespoons salad	1 green pepper, finely
oil	sliced
1 tablespoon vinegar	2 tablespoons
(wine or tarragon	chopped walnuts,
for preference)	optional
salt and pepper to	8 oz. cooked pork
taste	

1 Cook rice until just tender in plenty of well-salted, fast-boiling water, then drain very thoroughly.

2 Meanwhile, rub a large bowl with garlic, if wished, and in it mix together the oil, vinegar and seasonings.

3 Add the hot rice and mix thoroughly.

4 Stir in the remaining ingredients and lastly the pork, cut into bite-sized pieces.

5 Cover and set aside in a cool place for the flavours to blend.

6 When cold transfer to a serving dish.

Pork and cucumber salad

no cooking

you will need for 4 servings:

10–12 oz. cooked leg pork	4 lettuce leaves
½ cucumber	1 tomato

for the dressing:

¼ pint yoghourt	¼ teaspoon garlic salt
1 tablespoon chopped chives	1 teaspoon vinegar or lemon juice
¼ teaspoon dry mustard	salt and pepper

1 Cut the pork and cucumber into small strips.
2 Mix together in a bowl.
3 Prepare the dressing by mixing all the ingredients together just before using.
4 Toss lightly with the pork and cucumber.
5 Serve in cupped lettuce leaves.
6 Garnish with sliced tomato.

French dressing

no cooking

you will need:

1 teaspoon made mustard	little garlic salt, optional
good pinch salt and pepper*	2 tablespoons oil
good pinch sugar	up to 1 tablespoon vinegar or lemon juice

*A choice of peppers can be used, depending on the type of salad. If you want plenty of flavour, use a tiny pinch of cayenne as well as black or white pepper, or give a good turn with the pepper mill.

1 Put the mustard into a basin or on to a flat plate.
2 Add the seasonings and very gradually blend in the oil with the back of a spoon or fork until it has thoroughly emulsified with the mustard.
3 Add the vinegar or lemon juice.
4 If using garlic salt, this goes in with the seasonings.

Variations on French dressing

The basic French dressing can, of course, be varied in so many different ways.

Using less oil – if your meat salad is fairly rich in fat, i.e. if you are using pork or ham, you can use slightly less oil to give a sharper dressing.

With curry powder – a very little curry powder can be added with the seasonings to give a bite to a beef or rather strong-flavoured meat salad.

Mayonnaise

no cooking

you will need:

1 egg yolk	1 dessertspoon vinegar OR lemon juice
good pinch salt, pepper and mustard	1 dessertspoon warm water
up to ¼ pint oil	

1 Put the egg yolk and seasonings into a basin.
2 Gradually beat in the oil, drop by drop, stirring all the time until the mixture is thick. Stop adding oil when you find the mixture is creamy, otherwise the mayonnaise will curdle.
3 Beat in the vinegar or lemon juice gradually, then the warm water.
4 Use as soon as possible.

Note

If using an electric blender you can put the egg yolk, seasonings and vinegar or lemon juice into the goblet, switch on for a few seconds, then pour in the oil steadily.

Variations

Curried mayonnaise – blend 1–2 teaspoons curry powder with 1 or 2 tablespoons milk and stir in ¼ pint mayonnaise.

Horseradish mayonnaise – blend 1 tablespoon horseradish cream with ¼ pint mayonnaise.

Salad cream

cooking time: few minutes

you will need:

1 oz. flour	½ pint milk
1 teaspoon sugar	1 oz. margarine OR
½ teaspoon salt	1 tablespoon oil
good pinch pepper and dry mustard	1 egg
	2 tablespoons vinegar

1 Mix the flour, sugar and seasonings together with a little of the cold milk.
2 Bring the remainder of the milk to the boil, pour over the flour and stir thoroughly.
3 Put the mixture in the saucepan, adding the margarine or oil and the beaten egg.
4 Cook very slowly until the sauce coats the back of a wooden spoon.
5 Remove from the heat and whisk in the vinegar.
6 Pour at once into a screw-topped bottle.
7 Store in a cool place, it keeps for several days.

Ready-cooked Meats

The following gives a selection of the meats and salami sausages obtainable in good stores or grocers with delicatessen counters: all are excellent in salads or as hors d'oeuvre – allow 2–3 oz. per person.

Betz – a slightly more spiced type of salami.

Black pudding – a British sausage made with pig's blood, suet, breadcrumbs and oatmeal.

Brawn – a jellied British mixture of boned meat from pig's head.

Brisket – if pressed and glazed this is known as pressed beef. It is often salted, see page 70.

Belgian salami – a smoked, dried and well-seasoned pork and beef salami.

Cabanos – a very well-spiced garlic sausage.

Castalet – a slightly milder sausage.

Cervelat – a mild smoked pork sausage.

Chopped pork – a mild inexpensive luncheon meat.

Coarse-cut liver sausage – this is generally more spicy than the British liver sausage.

Continental liver sausage – this is generally more spicy than the British liver sausage.

Corned beef – a canned preparation of cooked pickled beef.

Danish salami – a rather salty pork sausage. Can be heated.

Extrawurst – an extra fine pork sausage, delicately seasoned.

Faggots – a country-type savoury dish with pork, pig's liver and kidney, now commercially made. Generally very good, see page 82.

Frankfurters – continental sausages to serve cold, or reheat.

French garlic sausage – a very highly seasoned sausage.

Garlic sausage – a high percentage of garlic, coarse-cut pork and ham. Serve cold.

German salami – mainly pork, reasonably mild. There are a number of varieties – Mettwurst, Tyrol sausage, Teewurst, Kerkawer, Kraatwurst and Bleuwurst.

Haggis – traditional Scottish dish made of liver, oatmeal, etc. Cook steadily in water for approximately 1 hour. Serve hot.

Ham – various grades of ham, both on the bone and pressed.

Ham sausage – a mild mixture of pieces and finely puréed ham.

Haslet – a commercial version, see page 82.

Hungarian salami – very mild, yet slightly sharp, pork salami.

Italian salami – these vary, some being rather finely minced meat with pieces of fat, others of coarser texture. Generally mild in flavour.

Jellied veal – veal set in a jelly like brawn.

Lachsschinken – this means 'salmon ham' because of its similarity in taste to smoked salmon.

Liver pâté – a paste of the foie gras type made from the liver of game, poultry or meat.

Liver sausage – a smooth-textured and inexpensive sausage.

Luncheon meat – this contains a variety of mild pork and ham, mixed.

Luncheon sausage – similar to luncheon meat, but round in shape.

Maryland ham – this is a particularly sweet ham, flavoured with honey.

Ox tongue – rolled and pressed, this can be bought sliced or in cans or glasses.

Paris ham – this is loin of pork devoid of any fat, then cured, smoked and cooked. Serve cold.

Parma ham – a very expensive, smoked ham. Generally served as an hors-d'oeuvre with pieces of melon.

Polish salami – a dried, somewhat highly seasoned, sausage of pork.

Polka suszona – as Polish salami.

Polony – an inexpensive sausage in red skin.

Pork boiling rings – a smoked sausage containing coarse-cut pork and seasoning. Eaten hot, sliced and fried, or boiled whole.

Pressed silverside – this is commercially pressed beef, see page 70.

Saveloy – an inexpensive British, fairly highly seasoned, red-skinned sausage. Serve cold or reheat.

Strasbourg liver sausage – this is pork blended with the liver.

Tongue sausage – this is finely minced tongue formed into a sausage shape.

York ham – this is considered Britain's best type of cured ham.

Galantines, Meat Loaves and Moulds

One of the most interesting ways to serve meat is in the form of a galantine, loaf or mould. It makes the meat go further and in many cases is the basis for two meals. When freshly cooked it can be served hot, and then later served cold with a salad. The quantities are for four, unless stated to the contrary.

Galantine

cooking time: 1¼ hours

you will need for 4 servings:

1¼ lb. stewing beef or pork	2–4 oz. fresh breadcrumbs
4 oz. streaky bacon	1 egg
1 good-sized onion	3 tablespoons stock
pinch mixed herbs	seasoning

1 Put the meat, bacon and onion through a mincer, blend with rest of ingredients.
2 Either put into a greased basin or loaf tin, or, for a round shape, a well-greased cocoa tin.
3 Steam or bake for approximately 1¼ hours in the centre of a very moderate oven (300–350°F. – Gas Mark 2–3).
4 Turn out and serve hot or cold.

Variations

With browned breadcrumbs – coat the container with a layer of browned breadcrumbs before putting in meat.

With a panada sauce – bind with a thick panada sauce, see page 84, using stock, tomato juice or milk instead of egg and stock.

With hard-boiled eggs – first put half the meat mixture into the container. Put 1 or 2 hard-boiled eggs over, then cover with the rest of the mixture.

Jellied meat loaf

cooking time: 3 hours

you will need for 4 servings:

1 knuckle veal	1 sliced onion
½ lb. pickled pork or salt belly pork	1 bay leaf
3 lamb's tongues	6 peppercorns
water, to cover	2 cloves
	2–3 sprigs parsley

1 Wash meat and cover with cold water.

2 Add onion, bay leaf, peppercorns, cloves and parsley.
3 Simmer gently for 3 hours.
4 Strain off the liquid and boil this rapidly until reduced to half.
5 Skin and slice the tongues and chop the other meat, removing all gristle and bones.
6 Pack this meat mixture in a wetted mould, pour the reduced liquid over.
7 Leave until cold and the jelly has set.

Faggots

cooking time: 1 hour 40 minutes

you will need for 4 servings:

6 oz. belly of pork	1 egg
12 oz. pig's liver	good pinch dried sage and thyme
1 pig's kidney (heart could be used)	OR ½–1 teaspoon each freshly chopped herbs
1 large onion	
seasoning	
2 oz. breadcrumbs	

1 Put pork, liver, kidney and onion into a pan with seasoning and water to half-cover.
2 Simmer gently for 40 minutes, then strain.
3 Mince or chop finely and blend with the other ingredients.
4 Form into balls and, if you can get a pig's caul (this is a membrane), wrap each ball in a piece.
5 If not, spread the mixture in a greased tin, mark into squares and cover with greased foil.
6 Bake for an hour in moderately hot oven (425–450°F. – Gas Mark 6–7).
7 Remove foil or caul before serving.

Haslet

cooking time: 1 hour

you will need for 4 servings:

1 lb. pork meat	1–2 oz. chopped fresh sage
1 lb. soaked bread crusts	pepper and salt to taste

1 Put the pork and bread through a very fine mincer.
2 Mix with the sage and seasoning and stuff into a 'pig's veil', i.e. the skin in which lard is encased, or wrap in greased foil.

3 Bake for about 1 hour in the centre of a moderate oven (375°F. – Gas Mark 4).

4 Serve hot or cold with a good gravy.

Cold sausage ring

cooking time: 40 minutes

you will need for 4 servings:

1 lb. pork sausage meat	½ teaspoon basil or sage
1 tablespoon tomato ketchup	2 slices bread, crusts removed
1 grated onion	1 beaten egg
¼ teaspoon celery salt	little dry sage and onion stuffing from packet
¼ teaspoon pepper	

1 Mix the sausage meat, ketchup, onion and seasonings together.

2 Soak the bread in the egg and then blend into the rest of the mixture with a fork.

3 Grease a 1-pint ring mould and coat with a little dry sage and onion stuffing.

4 Press the sausage mixture into this ring and bake (400°F. – Gas Mark 5) for 40 minutes.

5 Turn out and serve cold with salad.

Eating out of doors

Everyone has a hearty appetite when eating out of doors, and the following will be welcome. For a barbecue, make kebabs or cook chops, tomatoes and apple rings in one pan over a barbecue fire.

Cook jacket potatoes and vary these by blending the cooked potato pulp with butter and minced or chopped cooked ham and piling back in the case. Prepare interesting sauces for salads and desserts, and include plenty of fresh fruit.

Barbecues

Barbecued round of beef

cooking time: 55–70 minutes

you will need:

2 lb. round of beef	4 medium sized carrots
corn oil	
4 medium sized onions	Quick barbecue sauce (see page 86)

1 Brush round of beef on both sides with corn oil and brown over hot coals.

Potted pork

cooking time: 1 hour

you will need for 4 servings:

1 lb. roast pork	1 small minced onion
1 dessertspoon chopped parsley	¼ teaspoon powdered mace
a pinch grated nutmeg	salt and pepper
½ pint stock*	

*Make from simmering 1 pig's trotter or bones. When not using a pig's trotter, which helps to stiffen the stock, use just under ½ pint.

1 Cut the pork into small dice.

2 Mix together all the ingredients.

3 Press into a buttered casserole and cover.

4 Bake in oven (350°F. – Gas Mark 3) for 1 hour.

5 Leave in the casserole until quite cold.

6 Cut into slices for serving.

Variations

Beef – add 2 bay leaves and a small bunch of parsley when making the stock (omit nutmeg and mace). Dice or mince the meat.

Veal or lamb – add juice of half a lemon and a pinch of herbs to stock. Dice or mince the meat.

2 Place in sheet of double cooking foil, large enough to fold over roast; add quartered onions and carrots and coat with sauce. Fold foil over roast and cook on coals for 45–60 minutes, or until tender.

Mixed meat kebabs

cooking time: 10–15 minutes

you will need for 4–6 servings:

8 oz. rump or fillet steak	few tiny mushrooms
	butter
8 oz. lean lamb (cut from top of leg) or veal	

1 Cut the meat into small cubes and thread with the mushrooms on to four or more metal skewers.

2 Brush with melted better and cook under a hot grill, or over coals, until the meat is tender.

3 Serve on boiled rice with Quick barbecue sauce.

Variations

Using kidney and sausage – alternate halved

lamb's kidneys, halved sausages, small mushrooms, and rashers of bacon on skewers.

Using tomato and peppers – small whole tomatoes, sweet peppers, halved onions, etc. can be mixed in also.

Shish kebab – spiced – before grilling, brush the meat well with melted butter, then sprinkle with spices: ½ teaspoon saffron, ½ teaspoon powdered ginger, ½ teaspoon powdered cummin, good pinch cayenne and powdered cloves, pinch salt.

Shish kebab – marinated – to 1 lb. diced meat blend 3 tablespoons oil with 3 tablespoons wine, add a chopped onion, crushed clove garlic, seasoning, 2–3 crushed peppercorns (optional) and a little chopped parsley. Turn the diced meat in this for several hours, lift out and then cook as usual.

Jacket potatoes

Scrub large potatoes, wipe them dry, and rub with a little melted fat or oil. Place on a baking tray or on oven shelves and cook in a moderately hot oven (400°F. – Gas Mark 5) for 45 minutes to 1 hour. When done, cut a cross on top and add a nut of butter. Serve with a green salad.

Quiche Lorraine

cooking time: approximately 25 minutes

you will need for 4 servings:

2–3 rashers bacon	6 oz. cheese, grated
1 partly baked pastry case	seasoning
	to garnish:
2 eggs	parsley
¼ pint single cream	tomato quarters
¼ pint milk	

1 Chop bacon and fry very lightly.
2 Beat eggs, cream, milk, grated cheese, bacon and seasoning.
3 Pour into case carefully and bake in the centre of a moderately hot oven (400°F. – Gas Mark 5) until the filling is firm.
4 Garnish with parsley and tomato quarters.

Variation

Bacon quiche – halfway through cooking place thin bacon strips on top of quiche in a lattice design. Finish cooking and garnish with stuffed olives.

Sauces

Béarnaise sauce

cooking time: 20–30 minutes

you will need:

2 egg yolks	2–4 oz. butter
little cayenne pepper	1 finely chopped shallot
salt	
pepper	little chopped parsley
1–2 tablespoons lemon juice OR white wine vinegar	little tarragon vinegar

1 Put the egg yolks, seasonings and lemon juice or vinegar into the top of a double saucepan.
2 Whisk over hot water until sauce begins to thicken.
3 Add the butter in very small pieces, whisking in each pat and allowing it to melt before adding the next. DO NOT BOIL or the mixture will curdle.
4 Add the chopped shallot, parsley and tarragon vinegar.
5 A little cream can be added if it is too thick.

Brown sauce

cooking time: 8 minutes

you will need:

1 oz. cooking fat or dripping	¼ pint brown stock for panada or binding sauce OR
1 oz. flour	
¼ pint brown stock for coating sauce OR	1 pint brown stock for thin sauce
	salt and pepper

1 Heat the fat or dripping in a pan.
2 Add the flour and cook steadily in the fat until brown.
3 Be careful not to over-brown.
4 Add stock, stirring all the time, and bring to the boil.
5 Season and cook until thick and smooth.

Variation

With vegetables – Use 2 oz. of fat, and fry a little chopped onion, celery and carrot, for added flavour, and strain when cooked.

Cheese sauce

Use the ingredients and method for white sauce, see page 86. Stir in 3–4 oz. grated cheese, when the sauce has thickened. Be very careful not to over-cook the sauce, otherwise it becomes stringy and spoilt.

Espagnole sauce

cooking time: 45 minutes

you will need:

brown sauce, see page 84	1 carrot
few mushrooms	little smooth tomato pulp
1 rasher of bacon	sherry
1 onion	

1 Add chopped mushrooms, bacon, onion and carrot to the brown sauce.
2 Simmer until tender and sauce is very thick.
3 Sieve and re-heat with little smooth tomato pulp and sherry.

Variations

Madeira sauce – make as above, but add Madeira instead of sherry. Serve with ham.

Hunter sauce or Sauce chasseur – make as espagnole sauce above, but do not sieve.

Meat sauce (or Sauce bolognese)

cooking time: 1 hour 10 minutes

you will need:

1 onion	½ pint brown stock
2 skinned, chopped tomatoes	little red wine, optional
clove garlic, optional	pinch mixed herbs
1½ oz. fat	12 oz.–1 lb. minced beef*
1 oz. flour	seasoning

*The mince has a much better flavour and texture if it is *not* fried first, but added to the brown sauce.

1 Chop the onion, tomatoes and garlic finely and toss in the fat.
2 Work in the flour and cook for several minutes.
3 Add stock, bring to the boil and cook until thickened.
4 Put in the red wine.
5 Add the herbs, beef and seasoning and stir well.

6 Continue stirring until the meat is completely broken in small pieces.
7 Then lower the heat and simmer gently for 1 hour, stirring frequently.
8 This is the sauce that is served with cooked spaghetti, macaroni and rice or just in a border of creamed potatoes.

Onion sauce

Use the ingredients and method for white sauce, see page 86, then boil three onions, chop or slice and add to the sauce. Use a little onion stock in place of some of the milk, if liked. Or see recipe page 25.

Poivrade sauce

Use the ingredients and method for either the brown sauce, or better still the espagnole sauce, see left, add about 12 peppercorns and simmer in the sauce to give the pepper taste, strain and flavour with brandy.

Tomato sauce

cooking time: 30 minutes

you will need:

1 carrot	½ oz. flour
1 small onion	½ pint stock or liquid from can
1 rasher bacon	bay leaf
1 oz. butter	salt and pepper
5 large fresh or canned tomatoes	good pinch sugar

1 Dice the carrot, onion and bacon.
2 Heat butter and toss them in this, but do not brown.
3 Add tomatoes, simmer for a few minutes if using canned tomatoes or rather longer with fresh ones. Take time doing this since it improves the flavour of the sauce.
4 Blend flour with the stock and add the bay leaf.
5 Add to ingredients and simmer gently for about 30 minutes, stirring from time to time.
6 Rub through a sieve or beat with a wooden spoon.
7 Add seasoning and sugar.

Variation

Tomato brown sauce – use half brown stock and half tomato juice. Excellent in casserole dishes.

Bigarade sauce

cooking time: about 12 minutes

you will need:

½ pint brown sauce
rind 1 large orange
juice 1 orange
dessertspoon lemon
  juice

2 tablespoons claret
  or port wine
pinch sugar
seasoning

1 Make the brown sauce as recipe on page 84, being very careful not to over-season or to use a very dark brown stock.
2 Simmer the pared orange rind in the sauce, then strain.
3 Add the juice, port wine and pinch of sugar. Season very well.

White sauce

cooking time: 5–8 minutes

you will need:

1 oz. butter or
  margarine
1 oz. flour
½ pint milk for thick
  coating sauce OR

1 pint milk for thin
  sauce OR
¼ pint milk for panada
  or binding sauce
salt and pepper

1 Heat the butter gently.
2 Remove from the heat and stir in the flour.
3 Return to the heat and cook gently for a few minutes, so that the roux, as the butter and flour mixture is called, does not brown.
4 Add milk, bring to the boil and cook, stirring with a wooden spoon, until smooth and thickened.
5 Season well.
6 If any lumps have formed, whisk sharply.

Variations

Mushroom sauce – cook 2 oz. chopped mushrooms in the milk, then use milk to make white sauce. Add cooked mushrooms and reheat.

Horseradish sauce – whisk about 1 dessertspoon vinegar and 2 tablespoons grated horseradish into white sauce. Add a small amount of cream and a pinch of sugar.

Tartare sauce – (hot) (for veal) – make white sauce, then whisk in 2 egg yolks, 1 tablespoon cream, 1 tablespoon chopped gherkins, 1 teaspoon chopped parsley and a squeeze lemon juice. Cook gently for a few minutes without boiling. (Or use half gherkins and half capers.)

Parsley sauce (for gammon) – add 1–2 teaspoons chopped parsley and a squeeze lemon juice.

Apple sauce

cooking time: 20 minutes

you will need for 4 servings:

1 lb. apples
¼ pint water

1 tablespoon sugar
½ oz. butter or
  margarine

1 Peel, core and thinly slice the apples.
2 Put into a pan with the water, sugar and butter or margarine.
3 Cook gently until soft, then rub through a sieve or beat with a wooden spoon until smooth.

Quick barbecue sauce

cooking time: 25–30 minutes

you will need for 5–6 servings:

5 tablespoons olive
  or cooking oil*
1 medium onion,
  chopped
1 heaped tablespoon
  sugar
½–1½ tablespoons
  Worcestershire
  sauce (according to
  taste)

½–1 tablespoon mixed
  mustard, English or
  French
½ tablespoon salt
pinch pepper
juice of 1 lemon
6 tablespoons
  tomato ketchup
6 tablespoons water

*This amount of oil is excellent for keeping meat moist as suggested in the method, but it could be reduced to 2½–3 tablespoons if a less rich sauce is required.

1 Heat the oil and cook the onion in it until soft, then add remaining ingredients.
2 Simmer for 15 minutes. Makes ½ pint.
This is excellent for basting and serving with fried dishes, hot dogs, rissoles, hamburgers, etc.

Cumberland sauce

cooking time: 15 minutes

you will need for 4 servings:

¼ pint water (or half
  water and half wine)
grated rind and juice
  1 lemon
grated rind and juice
  2 oranges

1 teaspoon cornflour or
  arrowroot
2 tablespoons water or
  port wine
3 tablespoons
  redcurrant or apple
  jelly

1 Put water and fruit rind into a saucepan and simmer for about 5 minutes.
2 Strain if wished, then return liquid to pan. Finely grated rinds are very soft and look attractive

in the sauce. Add the fruit juice and cornflour or arrowroot, blended with the 2 tablespoons water or wine.

3 Bring to the boil and add the jelly. Cook until clear.

Offal

Offal is the name generally given to the internal parts of an animal but it does include the feet and ears.

Bones

Bones provide the basis for first-class stock, see page 17. The marrow from beef bones can be taken out and served as a savoury on toast. To re-heat the marrow from the bones of beef, just toss in a little butter.

Brains

Make a creamy white sauce, see page 86, add the brains from a calf's, pig's or sheep's head, and reheat for a few minutes. Flavour with a few drops of lemon juice. Serve on toast or as a sauce.

Calf's head with brain sauce

cooking time: 3 hours

you will need:

1 calf's head	bay leaves
parsley	brain sauce (see
mixed herbs	above

1 Split the head down the centre, wash well and remove brains.
2 Put ingredients in pan of cold water to just cover the head, bring to the boil, remove any scum.
3 Put on the lid and simmer gently for about 3 hours.
4 Take out all the meat and chop neatly. The tongue can be served separately or cut into neat fingers and added to the cooked meat.
5 Arrange the meat on a hot dish, pour over the brain sauce and garnish with snippets of crisp toast.

Chitterlings (fraise or crow)

This is the name given to the small intestines of a pig. They are sold ready prepared in some butchers and can be served cold, or fried in a little hot butter.

Feet or trotters

Calf's and pig's feet contain a great deal of gelatine and are used to help set moulds and brawn, see recipe below.

Ears

These are not so popular today, but were once considered a great delicacy. The traditional recipe in old country houses was to boil them until tender and serve cold.

Heads

The head of calf is considered the most delicate in flavour, but both sheep's and pig's heads can be used in exactly the same way. You will see that brawn can be made with a pig's head as well as feet, and a calf's head makes an excellent-flavoured brawn.

If using a sheep's or lamb's head, which does not contain as much natural setting quality as that of a calf or pig, you may need to dissolve 2 teaspoons of powdered gelatine in $\frac{1}{2}$ pint of the liquid at stage 7 of the brawn recipe.

Pork brawn

cooking time: 3 hours

you will need for 6–8 servings:

1 pig's head or	small bunch parsley
6 pig's trotters	water
2 bay leaves	8 oz. stewing beef or
seasoning	pork
pinch mixed herbs	

1 Split head, or the butcher will, down centre.
2 Wash carefully and remove the brains – the trotters just need washing.
3 Put into pan with all ingredients except the stewing steak or lean pork.
4 Simmer gently for 1½ hours.
5 Cool slightly, then dice the meat, including the skinned tongue.
6 Return to liquid with brains and the diced steak or pork, and simmer for further 1½ hours.
7 Arrange drained meat in mould or basin giving

good distribution of tongue and brains. Boil liquid until it is reduced to ½ pint.

8 Strain liquid over meat and allow to set.

Heart

The small heart of sheep, calf or pig can be stuffed and roasted. Ox heart is inclined to be tough and can be casseroled slowly. Use any of the recipes for casseroling or braising beef, but substitute heart or sliced ox heart instead.

Baked stuffed hearts

cooking time: 50 minutes

you will need for 4 servings:

2–3 sheep's hearts	OR
1 teaspoon salt	veal stuffing, see page
sage and onion	28
stuffing	2–3 oz. dripping or lard

1 Put the hearts into cold water with a teaspoon salt for about 20 minutes to draw out blood.
2 Dry the hearts well, then fill with stuffing. If you find it difficult, cut the hearts in halves, stuff, then put together again and tie with cotton.
3 Put into a roasting tin with the dripping and cook in a moderately hot oven (400°F. – Gas Mark 5) for about 50 minutes.
4 Cut into slices to serve.

Lights

These are the lungs of the animal. In some parts of the world they are considered a great delicacy when boiled slowly in a thickened sauce. They are generally bought for animal consumption.

Kidneys

These can be used in various ways, served either as a main dish or on toast as a savoury, with or without fried bacon. The kidneys from a pig, calf or lamb are all very tender and can be cooked fairly quickly.

To fry or grill kidneys

1 Wash and remove the skin.
2 Halve, if wished, and cut away any gristle.
3 Fry in a little butter or fat or brush with butter and put under a hot grill.

Ox kidney – substitute for beef or mix with beef in any of the casserole recipes.

Country kidneys

cooking time: 40 minutes

you will need for 2 servings:

4 lamb's kidneys	4 onions, chopped
2 oz. butter	4 oz. mushrooms,
½ lb. chipolata	chopped
sausages	seasoning
1 oz. flour	pinch mixed herbs
½ pint cider	

1 Halve the kidneys and brown in the butter.
2 Remove and lightly fry the sausages.
3 Stir in the flour and cook until golden brown.
4 Add the cider, kidneys and all the remaining ingredients.
5 Cover and simmer for 30 minutes.

Devilled kidneys

cooking time: 10 minutes

you will need for 2 servings:

8 lamb's kidneys	pepper and salt
2 oz. butter	toast
1 tablespoon vinegar	bacon
2 teaspoons mustard	

1 Gently fry the halved kidneys in butter for 8 minutes, turning.
2 Stir in vinegar, made mustard and a sprinkling of pepper and salt.
3 Cook 2 minutes more and serve on toast with bacon.

Kidneys in port wine

cooking time: 15 minutes

you will need for 4–6 servings:

12–16 lamb's kidneys	½ pint stock
2 oz. butter	bay leaf
1 small onion	¼ pint port wine
1 oz. flour	
seasoning	**to serve:**
	4 oz. long grain rice

1 Skin the kidneys and fry in the hot butter for a few minutes, together with the finely chopped onion – do not allow to brown.
2 Stir in the flour and seasoning and cook for several minutes, then blend in the stock and bring to the boil. Add the bay leaf and port wine and simmer gently for about 8 minutes.
3 Remove bay leaf and serve kidneys in a border of cooked rice.

Kidney ramekins

cooking time: about 40 minutes

you will need for 4 servings:

12 oz. potatoes	2 rashers fat bacon
little butter	ready-made mustard
1 tablespoon	1 rasher streaky
top-of-milk or cream	bacon, cut into 4
salt and pepper	parsley to garnish
3 large firm tomatoes	
3 lamb's kidneys	

1 Cook potatoes, mash well adding butter, top-of-milk or cream and seasoning. Line 4 ramekin dishes with potato and pipe a little around top edges.
2 Cut a slice off top of each tomato and scoop out seeds. Drain well and sprinkle inside with salt and pepper.
3 Skin, halve and core kidneys, cut bacon into small pieces and fry until crisp; divide between tomato cups.
4 Fry or grill kidney halves; sandwich together with a little mustard and place in cups.
5 Place a portion of streaky bacon on top of each. Put tomato cups in potato lined dishes and bake in a hot oven (425–450°F. – Gas Mark 6–7) until piping hot. Remove streaky bacon pieces before serving. Garnish with parsley.

Liver

This is one of the most important foods. It is not only extremely easy to digest, so that young children as well as the elderly can eat it, but it is an excellent source of iron.

Calf's liver is the most tender and easily digested and therefore suitable for grilling and frying. Lamb's liver or pig's liver can be substituted.

Ox liver is not suitable for quick methods of cooking. It should be casseroled gently.

Any of the casserole recipes can be used as a basis for a casserole of liver. Since the flavour is fairly strong, you may like to mix the liver with other meat.

Liver becomes tough as soon as it is overcooked, so do time the cooking most carefully. For most people it is more appetising if it is slightly underdone in the very centre, so being more moist and juicy.

To fry

Dust very lightly with seasoned flour, then cook gently for a few minutes only, on either side in plenty of hot butter or fat.

To grill

Brush well with melted butter or oil and cook steadily under the grill.

To steam

This is particularly easy to digest. Season lightly and cook between plates, with a little milk or butter, over a pan of boiling water.

Liver dumplings

cooking time: 30 minutes

you will need for 2 servings:

8 oz. liver	parsley
2 oz. breadcrumbs	1 egg
1 onion, chopped	flour
1 oz. butter	stock or water
salt and pepper	

1 Soak liver in cold salted water for an hour.
2 Drain and dry with a cloth.
3 Remove the filmy skin, cut the liver into small pieces and put it through the mincer twice.
4 Add breadcrumbs, onion fried in butter, salt, pepper, and plenty of finely chopped parsley.
5 Bind the mixture with an egg.
6 Flour the hands and form the mixture into small dumplings.
7 Roll them in flour.
8 Grease a shallow ovenware dish, arrange dumplings on it.
9 Cover barely level with boiling stock or salted water and cook in a moderate oven (365°F. – Gas Mark 4) for 30 minutes.
10 Serve with onion sauce, see page 85.

New ways to serve liver

Stuffed liver

Buy a thick piece of liver, preferably calf's. Split through the centre to give a 'pocket'. Put in stuffing, tie if wished. Either grill, fry or as the liver is thick, bake in the oven. Individual thickish slices can also be stuffed.

Liver pâté

Mince 1 lb. lamb's, calf's or pig's liver finely, blend with ½ pint white sauce and seasoning. Put into well-buttered dish, cover top with buttered paper and bake in a dish of water for approximately 45 minutes in very moderate oven (300–350°F. – Gas Mark 2–3).

Coarse-cut pâté

Mince liver coarsely, mix with $\frac{1}{4}$ pint sauce, finely diced uncooked bacon (about 4 oz.), add crushed clove garlic, 3 chopped gherkins, seasoning. Cover dish with bacon rashers and cook as pâté.

Creamed pâté

Mince the liver very finely, mix with $\frac{1}{2}$ pint white sauce, $\frac{1}{4}$ pint cream, 2 beaten eggs, seasoning. Cover with buttered paper and cook as liver pâté.

Liver with pineapple

Fry the liver in the usual way, dish up, then fry very finely chopped onion and slices of canned pineapple in fat remaining in pan.

Livage bake

Have liver cut into very thin slices, roll round skinless chipolata sausages. Arrange in dish with apple rings, season and sprinkle with powdered sage. Cover dish with buttered foil and bake for 25 minutes in moderately hot oven (400°F. – Gas Mark 5).

Liver pie

Liver can take the place of steak or other meats in pies; the cheaper ox-liver can be used.

Chinese pig's liver

cooking time: 10–15 minutes

you will need for 4 servings:

12 oz. pig's liver	1 small packet frozen
1 small cauliflower	peas
4 oz. mushrooms	1 tablespoon soya
2 oz. lard	sauce
4 oz. chopped cooked	salt and pepper
ham	$\frac{1}{4}$ pint stock OR
	$\frac{1}{4}$ pint water and stock
	cube

1 Cut the liver into thin slices.
2 Divide the cauliflower into two, and slice the mushrooms.
3 Heat the lard in a large frying pan, and fry the liver.
4 Add the cauliflower, ham and peas and fry gently for 5 minutes.
5 Add the soya sauce, mushrooms, seasoning and the stock.
6 Cook for a further 5–10 minutes.
7 Serve with creamy mashed potatoes.

Ox liver and prunes

cooking time: 45 minutes–1 hour

you will need for 4 servings:

$\frac{1}{2}$ lb. stoned soaked prunes	1–2 rashers streaky bacon
1 lb. ox liver	$\frac{3}{4}$ pint beef stock OR
1$\frac{1}{2}$ oz. flour	beef stock cube and
seasoning	$\frac{3}{4}$ pint hot water
1$\frac{1}{2}$ oz. butter	1 carton yoghourt
1 chopped onion	

1 Soak prunes overnight and remove the stones.
2 Cut the liver into 1-inch pieces.
3 Toss in seasoned flour.
4 Melt the butter in frying pan.
5 Brown the liver, onion and chopped bacon.
6 Pour on the beef stock.
7 Cover and cook gently on top of stove or in the centre of a very moderate oven (350°F. – Gas Mark 3) for 45 minutes–1 hour.
8 Pour over the carton of yoghourt and serve immediately.

Liver and apple casserole

cooking time: 1 hour 40 minutes

you will need for 4 servings:

1 lb. calf's liver	2 medium sized
1 oz. flour	cooking apples
seasoning	2 medium sized onions
1 teaspoon dry	6 rashers streaky
mustard	bacon
2 oz. fat	$\frac{1}{2}$ pint water

1 Cut liver into thin slices.
2 Mix together flour, salt, pepper and mustard and coat the slices of liver.
3 Brown lightly in heated fat.
4 Fill a greased casserole dish with alternate layers of liver, sliced and cored apples and onions, then top with pieces of bacon. Add water, cover and cook in a moderate oven (350–375°F. Gas Mark 4–5) for 1$\frac{1}{2}$ hours, removing lid for the last 20 minutes.
5 Serve with creamy mashed potatoes, mustard and spinach.

Liver soufflé

cooking time: 25–30 minutes

you will need for 4 servings:

1 small onion	6 oz. calf's or lamb's
2 oz. butter or	liver
margarine	seasoning
1 oz. flour	3 egg yolks
¼ pint milk	4 egg whites

1 Dice the onion and toss in the butter or margarine. Stir in the flour and cook for 2–3 minutes, then add milk, bring to the boil and cook until thickened.
2 Stir in the finely chopped raw liver, seasoning and egg yolks, and finely fold in the stiffly beaten egg whites.
3 Put into a greased 6-inch soufflé dish and bake in a moderate oven (375°F. – Gas Mark 4–5) until well risen and golden coloured. Do not overcook.

Serve at once.

Pig's fry

This is the term given to a selection of offal from a pig, i.e. heart, lights, liver, sweetbreads. Fry in a little fat for approximately 10 minutes until tender, or bake in a moderately hot oven (400°F. – Gas Mark 5) for 30 minutes, covering with fat and a little foil, if wished.

Sweetbreads

These are considered a great delicacy and provide an ideal food for invalids, since they are easily digested. They come from the pancreas, near the heart, and glands in the throat of a young calf, lamb or bullock. The pancreas is the least fine in quality. They must be used when very fresh.

Before using sweetbreads in any recipe they should be blanched. Put them into a pan of cold water. Bring the water to the boil. Then throw away the water and the sweetbreads will keep a very much better colour. You should then be able to take away the fine skin, when cool enough to handle.

Fried sweetbreads

cooking time: 20–25 minutes

you will need:

sweetbreads	egg
water	breadcrumbs
flour	fat for frying
seasoning	

1 Blanch the sweetbreads. Put into fresh, cold, salted water, bring to the boil and simmer gently for about 15 minutes.
2 Lift out of the water and when cool enough to handle, take off the fine skin. You may prefer to put the sweetbreads in a container under a weight to press and slice before coating, but this is not really necessary.
3 Coat with a little seasoned flour, beaten egg and breadcrumbs and fry until crisp and golden brown. Garnish with parsley and lemon.

Creamed sweetbreads

cooking time: about 20 minutes

you will need for 4 servings

1 lb. sweetbreads	seasoning
½ pint white stock OR	1 oz. flour
white stock and milk	2 tablespoons milk
little lemon juice	2 tablespoons cream

1 Soak the sweetbreads in cold water for 1 hour.
2 Put into a saucepan and cover with more cold water.
3 Bring the water to the boil and throw it away, this process is known as 'blanching' the sweetbreads, and whitens it.
4 Return the sweetbreads to the saucepan with the stock, lemon juice and seasoning.
5 Simmer gently for about 15–20 minutes.
6 Remove the sweetbreads and take off any skin.
7 Blend the flour with the milk, add to stock, then bring to the boil, add the sweetbreads and cook until thickened.
8 Lastly stir in the cream.

Variations

In pastry cases – creamed sweetbreads are an excellent filling for pastry cases, or they can be served on toast or in a ring of creamed mashed potato.

With mushrooms – the sweetbreads can be put into a white sauce with fried mushrooms for additional flavour.

Braised sweetbreads

cooking time: 1–1½ hours

you will need for 4 servings:

1 lb. sweetbreads	½ pint brown or espagnole sauce, see page 84

1 Prepare the sweetbreads by blanching and then remove the skin.
2 Put into either an espagnole sauce or brown sauce.
3 Simmer in a saucepan or transfer to a covered casserole and put in a very moderate oven (300–350°F. – Gas Mark 2–3) and cook for approximately 1–1½ hours until tender.
4 Serve with macedoine of vegetables.

Tail

Oxtail makes excellent casseroles. It can be braised as steak, see page 62, cutting the oxtail into convenient-sized joints.

Because some people find oxtail casserole very fatty, it is a good idea to cook it some hours before it is needed. Allow the dish to cool, remove any surplus fat and reheat.

Any stock left from cooking these casseroles can be diluted and used for a first-class soup.

Oxtail casserole

cooking time: about 3 hours

Use the ingredients as for Oxtail ragoût, see below, except use two-thirds stock and one-third red wine, and cook in a covered casserole for approximately 3 hours in a very moderate oven (300–350°F. – Gas Mark 2–3).

Oxtail ragoût

cooking time: 3–4 hours

you will need for 4 servings:

1 medium-sized oxtail	1 clove garlic, optional
1 oz. cornflour OR	4 carrots, sliced
2 oz. flour	1 small turnip, sliced
salt and pepper	2 sticks celery, sliced
little fat	14 oz. can tomatoes
4 oz. diced bacon, optional	1½ pints stock OR 2 beef stock cubes
2 medium-sized onions	and 1½ pints water
4 cloves, optional	1–2 leeks, sliced
bouquet garni	

1 Remove any excess fat from the oxtail and cut into serving pieces.

2 Blanch by covering with water and bringing to the boil. Drain and dry.
3 Coat the pieces in cornflour or flour, to which salt and pepper have been added.
4 Heat the fat in a pan and fry the pieces of oxtail and bacon until golden.
5 Pour off any excess fat from the pan, then add the onions stuck with cloves, *bouquet garni*, garlic and all vegetables except the leeks.
6 Add the stock or water and crumbled beef cubes.
7 Simmer for 3–4 hours; 30 minutes before the end of cooking time add the sliced leeks.

Tongue

A small tongue from a calf, sheep or pig can be used in exactly the same way as ox tongue. For cooking and pressing, see below, but tongue, when boiled and skinned, can be heated in a brown sauce, see page 84, or a Madeira sauce, see page 85, and served with vegetables.

Boiled tongue

cooking time: 2½–3 hours

you will need for 8–12 servings:

2 calf's tongues or 1 ox tongue	1 bay leaf salt and pepper
1 large onion	water to cover
2 pig's feet or ½ calf's foot, optional*	

*If omitting the pig's feet, which make the stock set, dissolve 2 teaspoons of powdered gelatine in stock at stage 6.

1 Trim the tongues, or tongue, of all horny parts. allow to soak in cold, fresh water overnight.
2 Drain. Place in a large saucepan together with the sliced onion, pig's or calf's foot, bay leaf, salt and pepper.
3 Cover level with water, bring to the boil and allow to simmer until the tongues are tender.
4 The time of cooking will obviously depend on the size of the tongues, but should be about 2½–3 hours for ox, or 1½–2 hours for calf's.
5 Allow to cool.
6 Boil the stock until reduced to one-third, or approximately ½ pint for the ox tongue and a little less for the calf's tongues.
7 Remove the skin and bones from tongues.
8 Roll in a cake tin or saucepan. Cover with drained stock.

9 Put a plate or weight over top to press into shape, and leave until cold.

10 Turn out when firm.

Tongue with grapes and almonds

cooking time: 2–2½ hours

you will need for 6–8 servings:

2 pints water	½ oz. flour
1 large onion	1 level dessertspoon
2 cloves	salt
bouquet garni	1 beef extract cube
seasoning	½ pint hot water
1 small ox tongue OR	1 oz. almonds
large calf's tongue	4 oz. white grapes
1½ oz. butter	(skinned and pipped)

1 Bring the water to the boil, add the onion stuck with cloves, *bouquet garni* and seasoning.

2 Add the tongue and simmer for 2–2½ hours until tender.

3 Remove the tongue and cool slightly.

4 Peel off skin and take out small bones at the root of the tongue.

5 Cut the meat in thin, lengthwise slices.

6 Melt 1 oz. butter in frying pan.

7 Add the flour and salt.

8 Stir in the beef extract cube dissolved in the hot water.

9 Stir until sauce boils.

10 Sauté the blanched, skinned almonds in the remaining butter.

11 Add the almonds to the sauce together with the sliced tongue and white grapes.

12 Serve very hot with creamed potatoes.

Tongue in Madeira sauce

cooking time: 15 minutes

you will need for 4 servings:

8 slices cooked	good ¼ pint Madeira
tongue	1 bay leaf
1 teaspoon	1 tablespoon
made-mustard	redcurrant jelly
1½ oz. butter or	seasoning
margarine	**to garnish:**
1 oz. flour	cooked or canned
¼ pint stock	peas

1 Spread the tongue very thinly with mustard.

2 Heat the butter or margarine in a large shallow pan. Stir in the flour and cook for several minutes, then gradually blend in the stock and wine. Bring to the boil, add the bay leaf and

simmer for 5 minutes, adding the jelly and seasoning well.

3 Put in tongue and heat for a few minutes. Serve on a large dish with peas.

Tripe

While many people dislike this intensely, it is a first-class food at a very economical price. It comes from the stomach of the animal. Tripe should be blanched before cooking as it improves the colour, see creamed tripe, below.

Creamed tripe

cooking time: 1¼ hours

you will need for 4 servings:

1 lb. tripe	1 oz. flour
water	½ pint milk
little lemon juice	little cream, optional
1–2 onions	1 oz. butter
seasoning	

1 Cut the tripe into neat fingers and put to soak in cold water for an hour.

2 Blanch by putting in a saucepan, just covering with cold water, and then bringing the water to the boil and simmering for a minute.

3 Throw the water away. Blanching both whitens the tripe and gives it a better flavour.

4 Add just enough water to cover the tripe, a little lemon juice, and the onions.

5 Season well and simmer gently for an hour. By this time the liquid will only be half covering the tripe.

6 Blend the flour with the milk, add to tripe, bring to the boil, and cook until thickened, stir in the cream and butter.

7 The tripe may be removed to a hot dish and the sauce cooked until it has thickened more.

8 The onion may be sieved and added to the sauce, if liked.

Variations

With egg – a beaten egg may be added to the sauce.

Tripe mornay – cook the tripe as Creamed tripe, then lift the meat on to a hot serving dish. Blend 3 oz. finely grated Cheddar cheese with the sauce and cook for a few minutes. Garnish with chopped parsley and paprika.

Tripe romaine

cooking time: 1 hour 20 minutes

you will need for 4–6 servings:

2 lb. dressed tripe
2 oz. butter
2 large, chopped
  onions
3 sliced leeks
1 chopped head
  celery
4 tomatoes
¼ pint dry white wine
  or cider
pinch nutmeg
seasoning
1½–2 oz. grated dry
  cheese

1 Blanch the tripe by covering it with water, bringing to the boil, then straining.
2 Melt the butter and gently cook the onion, leeks and celery until a pale gold.
3 Add the tripe, cut in fairly thin strips, and simmer for 10 minutes.
4 Skin, quarter and core the tomatoes.
5 Add them with the wine, or cider, nutmeg and seasoning.
6 Cover and cook very slowly for an hour.
7 Transfer to a shallow dish.
8 Sprinkle the cheese on top and put the dish under the grill to brown.

Trotters

This is another word for feet of the pig. They are excellent in a hotpot, or can be served in a parsley sauce.

Trotters in parsley sauce

cooking time: 1½ hours

you will need for 2 servings:

2 pig's trotters*
1 large onion
bacon rind, if available
water
½ bay leaf
salt
pepper
1 oz. butter or
  margarine
1 oz. flour or ½ oz.
  cornflour
1 tablespoon chopped
  parsley

*2 large or 4 small. Very rich, so only small amount used.

1 Scrub the trotters and place in a saucepan with the roughly chopped onion and the bacon rind.
2 Cover with water, bring to the boil and skim.
3 Add the ½ bay leaf and salt and pepper and simmer until tender.
4 Remove trotters and keep hot separately.
5 Strain the liquid and measure out ½ pint.

6 Make a sauce with the butter, flour, liquid and parsley and cook for 2 minutes.
7 Pour over the trotters and serve.
8 If wished a little milk could be added to the sauce in place of the liquid.

Fruited pork hotpot

cooking time: 2½ hours

you will need for 4 servings:

4 pig's trotters (hand
  or belly pork can be
  used)
1 oz. fat
1 oz. flour
¾ pint stock
1 good tablespoon
  concentrated
  tomato purée or
  tomato ketchup
seasoning
little sugar if using
  tomato purée
12 tiny onions or
  shallots
2 dessert apples (red)
2–4 oz. soaked prunes

1 Ask butcher to bone the trotters, if possible, and cut into thick slices. They can be cooked whole if preferred, or use about 1 lb. diced hand or belly pork.
2 Make a sauce of fat, flour and stock. Add the tomato purée or ketchup and seasonings.
3 Put the meat, onions, quartered apples (leave peel on for colour) and prunes in a casserole.
4 Pour over sauce and cover with a lid.
5 Cook for 2–2½ hours in very moderate oven (300–350°F. – Gas Mark 2–3).

Index